Alaska's
Evergreen
Lodge

on beautiful Lake Louise

Barney Sabo

Edited by Marthy Johnson
Photography by Judy Sabo and Larry Yahnian

Book design, typesetting: Vivencia Resources Group
Victoria, B.C. Canada   www.inetex.com/vivencia
Cover design: Roy Diment, VRG

National Library of Canada Cataloguing in Publication Data

Sabo, Barney, 1931-
 Alaska's Evergreen Lodge
 ISBN 1-55212-834-2
 1. Sabo, Barney, 1931- 2. Evergreen Lodge (Alaska)--History.
 3. Bed and breakfast accommodations--Alaska--Louise, Lake, Region.
 4. Louise, Lake, Region (Alaska)--Biography. I. Johnson Marthy W.
 II. Title.
 F912.L68S22 2001   979.8'3   C2001-911023-5

TRAFFORD

This book was published *on-demand* in cooperation with Trafford Publishing.
On-demand publishing is a unique process and service of making a book available for retail sale to the public taking advantage of on-demand manufacturing and Internet marketing.
On-demand publishing includes promotions, retail sales, manufacturing, order fulfilment, accounting and collecting royalties on behalf of the author.

Suite 6E, 2333 Government St., Victoria, B.C. V8T 4P4, CANADA
Phone   250-383-6864   Toll-free   1-888-232-4444 (Canada & US)
Fax   250-383-6804   E-mail   sales@trafford.com
Web site   www.trafford.com   TRAFFORD PUBLISHING IS A DIVISION OF TRAFFORD HOLDINGS LTD.
Trafford Catalogue #01-0234   www.trafford.com/robots/01-0234.html

10   9   8   7   6   5   4   3   2

Contents

Dedicated to my wife Judy and my daughter AnnMarie,
for their support in allowing me to accomplish my goals.

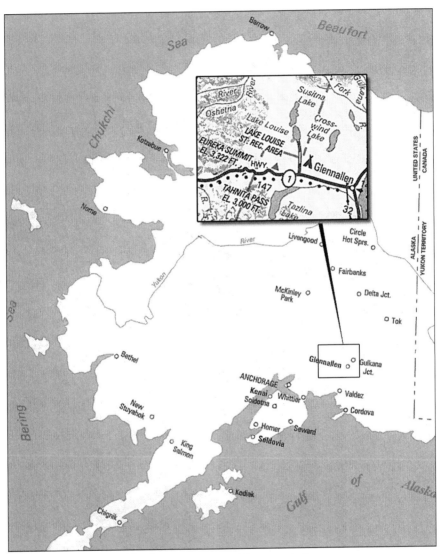

Alaska © AAA, used by permission

The Beginning

Life for me started in Brownsville, a small coal-mining town in western Pennsylvania on the Monongahela River about 40 miles from Pittsburgh.

My father, Joseph Sabo, had immigrated from a country in Europe now called the Slovak Republic. He came to the United States with a friend, and they both found work in the coal mines near Brownsville. His sister, Elizabeth, also immigrated into the United States and she married Andrew Cibrick, who owned a grocery store in an area we called "Hunkey Town."

My mother was born in the United States, but her parents took her back to the "old country" for several years before they returned. My parents were married when my mother and her parents returned to the United States, and my father continued to work in the coal mines. They lived in a company-owned house and purchased food and supplies from the company store. A few years later my father was fortunate enough to be able to buy a home that had been built for Elizabeth and Andrew Cibrick. The Cibrick store was not too far from my parents' new home and from then on they bought their groceries there.

We had six children in the family, three boys and three girls. Tough times were common, especially when the coal miners went on strike for months at a time. My parents were frugal; they grew a lot of their own vegetables and also had several peach and plum trees and a grape arbor. During the Depression my parents were able to feed the family by charging a lot of our food at the Cibrick store. When things got better, they paid for their groceries as they purchased them, and added as much as they could to pay off the old bill.

To help pay the bills, my older sisters Marie and Emma worked at the five-and-dime store, and my two older brothers, Joe and John, had jobs at the local soda pop shop and later at the gas station. When the war broke out in 1941, John enlisted in the Marine Corps and Joe in the Army. Marie had married Pete Jyachosky, Emma went to work in Cleveland, Ohio, building airplanes on an assembly line and my sister Teri was born this year.

I was ten years old, and earned a few dollars cutting the neighbors' grass and finding scrap metal I sold to the junk man, who came around on Saturdays to collect scrap metal for the war effort. Since most of the young guys had gone off to war, I got a few jobs hauling coal for our neighbors. The coal was usually dumped on the street; I hauled it in a 5-gallon bucket and stacked it in the neighbors' basement. Hauling five tons of coal for a neighbor once earned me twenty-five cents, enough for two tickets to the movies with five cents left over for a candy bar.

All of us attended St. Mary's Catholic parochial school, and were taught by the Sisters of Charity. Since I knew the alphabet and could count before I entered first grade, I was bored by reciting letters and doing work with numbers, so I refused to go to school. My brother John and sister Emma had to accompany me to school to make sure I got inside the classroom. As soon as the teacher turned her back, I was out of the door. When I got a head start the sister couldn't catch me, and if I got away I'd spend my time watching carpenters build a house or steamboats go up and down the Monongahela River.

The sisters got onto my scheme, and they assigned me a seat far away from the door. It didn't take me long to figure out that holding up one finger earned me a trip to the bathroom, and the sister wouldn't expect me back for a couple of minutes, and holding up two fingers gave me even more bathroom time.

Over time, I received quite a few lickings and other punishment for missing school, but I just couldn't stand the repetition. I can still picture Sister Benedict, the principal, giving me a lecture in front of grades one and two. She told me I was intelligent, but since I had not attended school regularly, I was going to flunk first grade. I repeated first grade and did graduate from St. Mary's.

What I learned about discipline and respect while attending this school has served me well during my lifetime. I went through several football camps with twice-a-day practices and an eight-week program with the 101st Airborne for my basic training. The camps and basic training were relatively easy compared to the nine years of teaching and punishment by the Sisters of Charity. The sisters had it made, because if I went home and told my parents what the sister had done to me that day, I'd get punished again at home for being disobedient at school.

The sisters had several methods of punishment. At times we had to do our math problems or sentence diagramming on the blackboard. After we finished our work on the blackboard we were required to stand at attention with our hands behind our backs. The sister looked over our work and if we'd done a good job she'd write our grades on the blackboard. If we'd done the problem incorrectly the sister would grab the hair on the front of our heads and bounce our heads against the blackboard a few times.

Another form of discipline–or torture–the sisters used involved a ruler or a long green stick such as a florist uses to stake plants. The sisters had some predetermined punishment for different infractions. A cuss word would get us hit across the palm of each hand with a ruler or with this long green stick. If we flinched on either stroke, the sister started the count over again for each hand.

A third form of the sisters' discipline required that we put our fingers together with the fingernails of each hand pointing upward. With a ruler the sister then whacked us several times on the fingertips. If you think that doesn't hurt, try it on your own hand. Again, if we flinched the count started over. If I learned anything from this punishment it was to keep my fingernails short. I keep them short to this day.

Several years later I attended a graduation ceremony for George Behary, a friend of mine, at St. Vincent's college in Latrobe, Pennsylvania. At the ceremony I met Sister Mary Frances, one of the sisters who'd taught and beat the hell out of me at St Mary's Catholic School. I asked the Sister if she remembered me and she said, "How could I forget you!" Next I asked her if she remembered working me over with a blackboard pointer. She said if she did that, I probably deserved it. So I told her I was bigger than she was now, and what would she do if I turned her over my knee and gave her a good spanking? She glared at me and said, "You wouldn't dare." Then she walked away.

The sisters tried their best to get me to continue my education in a Catholic high school, and they wanted me to become a Trappist monk. That life did not appeal to me, and I attended a public high school. My first year there was an eye opener. The lack of discipline and the lack of respect students had for teachers amazed me. I coasted through most of my classes because what they were teaching I had learned from the sisters the previous year.

I graduated from Brownsville High School in 1950. For several years I played football, and I was good enough to make the Big Five and the All-County conference teams. I ran track and acted as co-captain of the track team for four years and set a record in the 400 yard dash that held up for several years.

In my senior year I received scholarship offers from the University of Pittsburgh, William and Mary, Wake Forest, and Temple. I visited Wake Forest and William and Mary and decided to attend the latter. While playing freshman football I reinjured the cartilage and ligaments in my right knee.

Before each practice and before each game the trainer coated my knee with tincture of benzene and used adhesive tape to stabilize it. After practice or game I removed the tape and noticed that every time I took off the tape a few pieces of skin came off, too. After several weeks of this routine my knee and leg started to look pretty ugly, and I developed an allergic reaction to the adhesive tape. The team doctor offered no solution to my problem. It appeared that my football career was over and I lost interest In college. After the first semester I dropped out.

I went to work as a laborer in a local boat-building yard and was given the opportunity to attend the welding school offered by the company. I worked at the marine yard until I received my draft notice from Uncle Sam. After taking a battery of tests, I was interviewed by a representative of the Army Security Agency. He told me that if I enlisted for a three-year hitch I'd have the opportunity to attend a special training school for at least a year, and upon graduation I'd have a choice of my overseas assignment.

I enlisted for three years and after eight weeks of basic training with the 101st Airborne at Camp Breckenridge, Kentucky, I was assigned to Camp Gordon, Georgia. After graduating from cryptography school there I was given the choice of three overseas assignments–Germany, Alaska, and Korea. I picked Germany because George Behary, my Catholic godfather, was stationed there. However, I was not allowed to go to Germany because I had a top secret and crypto clearance and I had a lot of relatives in nearby countries.

I'd always wanted to hunt and fish in Alaska, so that was my next choice. I was stationed there for approximately two years, and thoroughly enjoyed the state. Although I wanted to return and live in Alaska, I knew the summers were beautiful, but the winters were severe. If I was going to return I needed a profession that would allow me to work inside during the winter, and leave me some free time during the summer months. Teaching school seemed to fit my plan to a T.

After my discharge from the Army Security Agency I enrolled at San Jose State College in San Jose, California. Because I'd always been handy with woodworking tools, I enrolled in the industrial arts program. When I was a kid, my parents didn't have money for toys, so I'd made my own out of the wooden orange crates I got from my aunt's grocery store.

Upon completion of my first year in college I returned to Alaska for the summer to work at Seldovia Bay Packing Company. I worked for a Mrs. Boyette in the commissary, and learned that her husband, John, was a bush pilot. John took me flying a few times, and he gave me a few flying lessons in a tandem-seated Taylorcraft. From that time on I knew I wanted to learn how to fly an airplane. I worked my regular hours in the commissary but also drove a dump truck in my spare time to make some extra money to buy a newer car.

In the fall I returned to San Jose and things did not go well. My brother John died of a kidney ailment, and I was devastated. He was only five years older than I. We'd been very close, and he was the one who'd encouraged me to move to California to continue my education.

I had planned to return to Alaska to work in the cannery for the summer, but after John's death I decided to stay in Merced to help my sister-in-law, Charleyne, and her young daughter, Cristy. Charleyne helped me get a job driving a beer truck for the summer. It paid well, but the temperatures in Merced can climb to 100 degrees during the summer, and my system was geared to the weather in Alaska.

I returned to San Jose in the fall for my junior year. To make ends meet I worked as an ID checker and bouncer in Me & Ed's pizza parlor. It was a fun job and I got to meet a lot of people. I also had the opportunity to eat a few pizzas and drink a few beers. During the summer I took a few classes at San Jose and got a job teaching driver's training to adults. Teaching adults to drive in a big city provided me with some exciting days and prepared me for my first year of teaching.

Upon graduation from San Jose State College in 1959 I received a job offer from the Merced School District. I accepted the offer and the first year I taught basic math, driver's training, arts and crafts, and two classes in woodworking. I coached football after school and was also elected president of the faculty association.

During the summer months I worked construction and during the school year I attended night classes to work on a master's degree in secondary school administration. C. J. Groves was our assistant principal. He was not only a well-educated person but he had a personality that made him successful with students and teachers alike. C.J. Groves was my inspiration to become an assistant principal.

After five years of teaching I requested a year's leave of absence so that I could return full-time to Fresno State College to finish my master's degree. To earn some money prior to going back to school I worked as a park ranger in Yosemite National Park, assigned to the Crane Flat area as a patrol officer.

One night, my partner, Doug, and I went down to the valley floor of the park to drink a couple of beers and have a pizza. We were both on patrol the next day, but since we didn't feel too good we didn't want to stop anyone for a traffic violation. We cruised the roads for a while, and decided we'd better pull off and take a nap.

After an hour or so we heard a car coming up the road with the volume of the radio turned up fairly high. The car was a Corvette convertible with the top down, and the lady driving it was the sister of my partner's girlfriend. I knew she was a nurse and her name was Judy, since I had seen her at the hospital when my partner and I'd brought in a young couple who'd had a life-threatening experience with a hibachi. They'd cooked their steaks on it, and after dinner they'd taken the hibachi into their tent to keep them warm. Luckily, after a while the lady had to go to the bathroom and when she got up she felt dizzy. She crawled out of the tent and when her head cleared a bit she dragged her husband out of the tent and asked the people camping next to them to go for help.

Since we didn't have much in our log book for the day, we decided to give Judy a ticket for making too much noise in a National Park. We looked up the park regulations, and they did state that it was illegal to make loud or excessive noise in the park.

I drove the patrol car up behind Judy's car and turned on the siren and the rotating beacon. She pulled over to the side of the road and I walked up and asked her for her driver's license and registration. About the same time our boss, Homer Leach, pulled up to see what was going on. Judy had been up most of the night helping Homer's wife, Beth, with the delivery of their first child.

Homer asked what was going on and I explained to him about the noise that was against park regulations. Homer told Judy that these two rangers knew the park regulations, and he would talk to her about it at a later time.

After Homer left I told Judy that if she would go to dinner with me at Evergreen Inn, I'd forget about the ticket. She agreed to that, and a few months later we were married in Las Vegas, Nevada. Judy continued to work as a nurse in Yosemite for the next several months while I kept working toward my master's degree.

Upon completion of my degree I applied to various chool districts for the position of assistant principal, and went to several interviews. I was particularly impressed with my interview with Dr. Dafoe of the Anchorage School District.

The Anchorage Borough School District hired me as an industrial arts teacher and administrative trainee. After just a few months the principal of our school was killed in a small-plane crash, along with another high school principal. I was promoted to the position of principal in the spring of 1965.

Being promoted to principal of a brand-new school is a challenge in itself. I was advanced to the position after only about seven months with the school district. Not only was I the new kid on the block, but I was also moved ahead of a lot of teachers who had worked for the State of Alaska, and the assistant principal, who had worked for the Anchorage Borough School District for several years.

A lot of grumbling was going on in the community and among the staff. Thank goodness for the excellent professors I had had at Fresno State College. What I'd learned in the secondary school administration classes served me well in dealing with this difficult situation. The Anchorage Borough School District had just taken over Chugiak High School, which had been built by the State of Alaska. Several of the people working in the school district administration office were helpful during this transition period. Bob Hall, our personnel director, was especially helpful and was able to find some well-qualified teachers for my staff. Dr. Dafoe, the superintendent who'd hired me, also gave valuable assistance during the transition.

The following summer I designed a house and supervised its construction. My wife didn't know the difference between a two-by-four and a two-by-six, but I asked her to be the inventory control person and she did an excellent job of checking the loads of lumber and other supplies that were delivered to the site.

After my third year as principal of Chugiak High School I asked for a transfer to a junior high school. As a principal I was required to be present at all the functions that took place at the school or my assistant principal had to be in attendance. Our daughter, AnnMarie, was just a year old and I wanted to spend more time with the family. I also wanted to have some time to go hunting, fishing, and flying my Super Cub.

My transfer request was granted and I was assigned to Romig Junior High School in Anchorage. Romig was a fairly new school with around nine hundred students and forty-two staff members. I really enjoyed working with the teachers and students there. Most of the student activities were held during the school day, so I had time to spend with my family, and time to go hunting, fishing, and flying.

Meanwhile, I had passed the test for a private pilot's license, and had accumulated quite a few hours flying a Cessna 150. That plane is equipped with tri-cycle landing gear, and it is not suitable for landing anywhere except on a relatively smooth surface. Since I wanted to hunt moose and caribou I wanted an airplane that could be used to land on the sandbars of a river or on a surface that wasn't too smooth.

I purchased a 90-horsepower Super Cub, commonly called a tail dragger. The Super Cub is equipped with regular landing gear but it also has a tail wheel instead of a nose wheel, which makes it easier to land on a rougher surface. Instead of the control wheel used on the Cessna 150 and other aircraft, the Super Cub is equipped with a control stick.

I found an instructor, Ed Broome, who was proficient at teaching people how to fly this plane. The Cessna 150 and the Super Cub are quite similar when it comes to takeoff and flying. Landing a Super Cub is a different story. Screwing up the landing of a Cessna

150 can be a very scary and sometimes a forgiving experience. If you screw up landing a Super Cub, quite often you will end up in a ground loop or worse. A ground loop consists of spinning around like a top upon landing the aircraft.

I can speak about ground loops from experience. Ed Broome gave me a few hours of instruction in my Super Cub, and I had the plane outfitted with a set of large beach tires. Ed told me to be very careful when landing a Cub in a crosswind, since it has a tendency to ground-loop.

Judy decided to come to Merrill Field in Anchorage to watch me fly my new Super Cub. I made a couple of touch-and-go's commonly known as takeoffs and landings, and felt pretty comfortable flying my new plane. On my third landing, however, I did not compensate for the crosswind coming from my left, and when I touched down on the runway the plane went into a ground loop. There was not much I could do except shut off the switches. I was heading for a twin-engine aircraft that was tied down near the runway. Thank goodness my Cub stopped spinning before it hit that plane.

The control tower called on the radio and asked if I was okay. I don't know how long it took me to answer, but I told him I was fine. Several people came out to help me move the plane off to the side of the runway. The only damage to the airplane was a blown tire and a scraped wing tip. It's a common saying among pilots that any landing you walk away from is a good landing.

Needless to say I didn't feel I had made a good landing. Judy had arrived at Merrill Field just about the time I took off for my third touch-and-go. She saw the plane go into the ground loop and didn't know if I was injured or not. She hadn't been too excited about my flying an airplane in the first place, so I told her I would take some additional flying lessons in the Super Cub.

Judy enrolled in a class for the wives of the pilots called the 99'ers or Powder Puffs. I kept my Cub at Birchwood airfield, and Judy took some flying lessons and learned how to operate the radios in the plane. I practiced short-field takeoff and landing at Birchwood and at times I flew across Cook Inlet to look over the area around Big Lake, and on to Palmer to fill up with gas before returning to Birchwood.

Super Cub on wheels

I had scheduled the annual inspection on the Super Cub, and after the inspection I planned to fly over to Big Lake. I took off from Birchwood, which was a gravel strip with no control tower, and set my course for Big Lake, which would take me across Cook Inlet. Just as I started across the inlet I noticed that the RPM gauge was not moving. My first thought was that the engine had quit, and I was going to be forced to land in the water. I revved up the engine and could hear it accelerate, and the prop was turning, so I decided I was going to turn back toward land, hoping to make it back to the airstrip. This is not what I had been taught to do, but I didn't want to land in the water, especially in the strong tides of Cook Inlet.

I made it back to the airstrip, made a good landing, and taxied my airplane to my tie-down spot as I tried to figure out what had happened to the RPM gauge. Nothing seemed to be wrong with it, but it wouldn't work. The mechanic who worked on my airplane came out to inspect the plane and found that he had put a crimp in the RPM cable. The gauge worked just long enough for me to run up the engine to check the magnetos, and it lasted until I started my flight across Cook Inlet. Needless to say I did not have kind words for this mechanic, and I changed to another one soon afterward.

Cessna 150

The Decision

I was enjoying life. I had a good job with thirteen years' experience. I'd worked hard to put myself through school; I was in Alaska, and I had just returned from a beautiful trip to Europe with my family and my wife's parents. I had just purchased a Mercedes in Europe, and I owned my own airplane.

Most people would have been satisfied to have accomplished any one of these goals, but something or someone kept telling me I was going to operate a business that provided recreation for a lot of people. In my mind's eye I pictured a very large area, where people would come to enjoy themselves.

We drove around Alaska looking at businesses that were for sale, but nothing seemed to fit the description of the place in my dream, or vision. In December I saw an ad in the Anchorage newspaper, which advertised a lodge for sale at Lake Louise, Alaska. After I told my wife about it, we decided to drive up to the lake, which is about 180 miles from Anchorage.

When we arrived at the lodge we were a bit surprised to find such a rustic place. A few people were drinking coffee in the lodge, and talking about flying, ice fishing, and hunting for caribou. The lodge owner was Doc Pease, a slightly built fellow with a full beard, and quite a few of his teeth were missing. We decided to look around a little more, and I asked Doc's wife, Kay, if we could stay overnight. They had a vacancy, and she told us we could have the trailer close to the lodge.

The trailer turned out to have an oil heater and a double bed located in the back quite a distance from the heater. Thank goodness we'd brought my down construction parka and Judy's fur parka. Our daughter had her down parka and her mukluks. We ended up sleeping with all our clothes on, and two sleeping bags on top of us. We also tucked our daughter between us.

The heater was turned up to its highest setting, and I was afraid it would overheat and set the trailer on fire. I told Judy that if the trailer caught on fire there was no way we could get out, since the heater was next to the door. In case of fire she'd have to help me kick out the large window next to our sleeping area.

We made it through the night without any problems, and the next morning we had breakfast in the lodge, which had no running water, or even a restroom. We had a cup of coffee and ordered breakfast, but the counter could seat only five people at a time, so we had to wait our turn.

Sitting on the couch in the lodge I couldn't figure out why I could feel a cold draft on the back of my neck, especially since the huge oil-burning stove was cherry red hot. As I turned to watch a plane land on the runway, I found out where the cold air was coming from. The windows were single pane, and the spaces between the logs were at least half an inch wide.

The lodge was built on a hill overlooking Lake Louise. The view was beautiful, though somewhat marred by several doghouses Doc had used for his team. The shelters were in bad shape, and the dogs' residue didn't help the view.

When we were ready to leave, the Mercedes wouldn't start. It was 45 degrees below zero. Doc Pease used his propane torch and a piece of flexible pipe to heat up the engine and the battery, and after a while the car started and we headed back to Anchorage. On the way home we discussed what could be done to make the lodge attractive, and how we could improve on the service. The setting was right, but the atmosphere and the service needed a lot of help.

We went back a couple of times to look around and ask more questions about the business and the surrounding area. Doc, we were told, wanted to sell because the army and the air force had closed their recreation sites on Lake Louise, and business was not very profitable. We also found out that Doc had a drinking problem, and that Kay had closed the liquor store for that reason. In-cluded in the sale of the business was an air taxi permit, a permit to sell liquor, a small marina, a couple of gas pumps, and forty acres of land.

As we drove out to the highway from the lodge we passed two beautiful evergreens, and we decided that if we purchased the business we would call it Evergreen Lodge. The restaurant where I'd taken Judy after almost giving her a ticket for making noise in Yosemite National Park was Evergreen Inn.

For several weeks we debated the pros and cons of giving up the relatively secure future with the school district versus moving to a remote area with a young daughter, and venturing into business. My colleagues thought I was foolish to give up a career I had worked so hard for. The time to make a decision was getting critical. It was only fair to give the school district ample time to find a replacement for me, and I wanted to purchase the lodge in the spring before the summer tourist season started.

I knew what I wanted to do, but I still struggled with the idea of giving up the security of a thirteen-year career and going off to live in the bush. When I called my father-in-law, a person I respected, and told him what we were contemplating, he told me, "If you don't do it you may be sorry about it for the rest of your life." That was the clincher. We decided to purchase the lodge and start a new chapter in our lives.

We closed the deal on the purchase, and I turned in my resignation to be effective on May 15, 1969.

When we told my flight instructor, Ed Broome, about our plans he said Meese would really like the lodge. I thought he was being funny by saying *meese* as a plural for *moose*, but he explained that Meese was his wife, and she had a lot of experience cooking at various ski resorts. We had known Ed for at least two years, and that was the first time we heard he was married.

We finally met Meese, and she agreed to help us pack up the house and come to work for us as a cook's helper. Things got hectic, because we had to sell our new home and wind up my duties as assistant principal. We sold the Mercedes and ordered a four-wheel-drive pickup truck from a dealer my brother Joe knew in Merced, California. My wife's brother Ward and my nephew Kurt agreed to drive the truck to Alaska. I sold the 90-horsepower Super Cub and bought a 125-horsepower Cub on floats. It came with a set of skis for winter flying.

About twenty people agreed to help us with the move to the lodge. Some of them were neighbors, but most were teachers who'd worked with me at Chugiak High School and Romig Junior High. Bob Perry, an attorney, and his wife, Linda, also volunteered to help with the move. We loaded the moving van in the evening, and started out on the road the next morning. Only a few miles from the house the truck overheated. We called the rental company and they came out and fixed a broken fan belt. By the time we arrived at the lodge all our help had made themselves at home. Some had brought food, so we combined our food supplies and had our first meal at our new lodge.

Everyone jumped in to help clean up the inside and the grounds outside. After a while the number of empty whiskey bottles, found in the most unusual places, became a joke.

Doc Pease

On the day we moved to the lodge Doc Pease showed me how to check the generator that supplied power to the lodge, and how to determine how much was left in each fuel tank. He also showed me how to fill the different sizes of propane containers.

Doc told me he was going to build his home across the lake, and he'd give me the job of freighting the lumber and supplies over to his building site. Three days later Doc surprised me by saying he was going to take his business to Lake Louise Lodge. In our previous discussions he'd had nothing good to say about the place.

Doc built his home across the lake and it goes without saying that I didn't get to freight any materials to his building site. One summer night not long after we bought the lodge I heard some noise in the lower parking lot where a few of Doc's customers kept their trailers. I got dressed to check things out, and found the customers hooking up their trailers. The next day I found out that Doc's former customers had moved their trailers to Lake Louise Lodge.

It appeared we were not going to get any support from Doc in promoting the business, so I told Judy we'd better learn about the lodge business on our own. When people found out that Doc was not around the place, strange things began to happen. More customers came into the lodge to see the new addition and to use the indoor bathrooms. Several customers told us they had quit coming in because they didn't want to be around Doc when he was drinking. I wasn't happy with Doc and his decision to move his business to our competition, but in the long run he did us a favor by not being around our place.

Every now and then Doc got on the citizens band radio and asked Ruth at Lake Louise Lodge if she wanted to fly over to the secret silver salmon lake to go fishing. I had asked Doc to show me his secret lake, but he refused. The Department of Fish and Game didn't want anyone to know the location, he said. This really bugged me. I bought the lodge from Doc, and yet he wouldn't tell me about any good fishing spots.

I told Judy that the next time Doc got on the CB radio to invite Ruth to go fishing with him to give me a call, no matter what I was doing. While I was working on the docks one day Judy called to tell me Doc was planning to go fishing on the secret lake. I stopped what I was doing and did a preflight on my Super Cub. When Doc landed on floats at the competitor's lodge I was ready to take off after him.

Doc had a PA-11 with a 90-horsepower engine. I had a 125-horsepower engine, so I could fly perhaps a little faster than Doc. I followed him after his takeoff, climbed above him, and trailed him to his secret lake. After he landed I gave him a buzz job, marked the lake on my map, and flew back to the lodge. We flew quite a few people to this lake, since it provided excellent fishing for landlocked salmon in the summer and also in winter.

Judy's mom and dad came to the lodge every summer to spend three weeks or so with us. Her dad took AnnMarie fishing for grayling on a small lake near the lodge. Both of them caught quite a few and Judy cooked them for supper.

Every time I had to fly somewhere around the lake system I asked Judy's dad, Mac, if he wanted to go with me. He always responded, "No, I don't want to go with you–you will probably crash." Several times he told us the story of flying over the Grand Canyon in his younger years in a Ford tri-motor, and it had really scared him, He wasn't fond of flying.

One day I had to fly down the lake system to Tyone Mountain Lodge, and I asked Mac if he wanted to come. He completely surprised me by saying yes, he wanted to go. We got him set up with a pair of hip boots and a baseball cap. I taxied away from the docks and climbed out over Lake Louise, telling Mac to look down at the beautiful island we were flying over. No answer came, so I turned around to tell him about the view, and all I could see was a pair of hands holding up a spread-out newspaper. I finally got him to put down the paper, and I showed him a few more interesting spots around the lakes.

Super Cub on floats

We landed at Tyone Mountain Lodge and went inside for a cup of coffee and a piece of pie. After we took off again I showed Mac some caribou swimming across the lake, flew around a little more, and started to head back to the lodge. When Mac found out where we were going, he told me, "Don't be so cheap. Let's fly around a little more." He promised to buy me some gas when we got back to the lodge. After that trip Mac was hooked on flying, and he wanted to fly every chance he got.

I didn't have a commercial license, so I couldn't charge a fee for flying on our air taxi permit. I hired a commercial pilot who was certified to fly single-engine land and he also had his float plane rating. This gentleman flew for us until the second moose hunting season opened in November.

New Addition

The restrooms in the old part of the lodge consisted of two chemical toilets similar to the toilets you'd find in a motor home or a trailer, and they were usable only during the summer months. Instead of having a holding tank to catch waste products, Doc had dumped the waste over the hill toward the lake. This did not appeal to me at all, since the lake water was pumped from the lake to the lodge to be used for drinking and cooking.

During the winter months, the water used at the lodge also came from the lake, but someone had to drill a hole through the ice, scoop the water into a large, galvanized can, and haul it up to the lodge. Kay Pease was frugal with water, and the waste water was thrown out the back door of the kitchen.

The water and sewage systems were the number one priority in changes I wanted to make as soon as possible. Prior to the purchase of the lodge, I had drawn up a set of plans that would double the size of the establishment. Gene Needles was a local guide and outfitter who also built log homes and cabins. He agreed to build the lodge addition and find a plumber to help me install new water and sewage disposal systems.

Gene and his crew did an excellent job building the addition and remodeling the older part of the lodge. He used 6-inch dry spruce logs that were flat on top and bottom and on the inside and installed a vapor barrier and 3 inches of insulation. The inside walls throughout the older and newer parts of the lodge were paneled with ¾ inch tongue-and-groove paneling. This gave the lodge a rustic but clean-looking interior. The addition included a shower, men's and ladies' restrooms, and a full basement.

The construction crew worked hard lifting and fitting the 6-inch logs into place. Judy let Meese prepare lunch for the workers to see how she'd work out as a cook's helper. Meese served us tuna fish sandwiches and a soup so thin it looked like boiled water with parsley on top. After lunch I told Meese Gene's crew worked hard, and they needed a substantial lunch. From that day on Judy supervised all meals served at the lodge. Meese helped Judy in the kitchen for several more weeks, and then decided to return to Anchorage.

The plumber and I worked on the new water and sewage disposal systems. I hired a backhoe operator to dig a trench from the lodge to the lake, because I planned to pump water from the lake for our water supply. I had worked on the installation of a typical septic tank and drain field system on the house we'd sold in Chugiak, so I felt confident that the same system would work here.

The backhoe operator dug the hole for the septic tank, and a sizable hole for the log crib I planned to use for the drain field. He dug down to a depth of 12 feet and hit a solid barrier of frozen earth. Still, I didn't expect any problems with the drain field, since all the material he'd excavated was loose gravel about ¼ to ½ inch in size.

The left-over material we used to backfill around the lodge basement. I used two ¼ inch thaw cables on the incoming water line, plus 3 inches of rigid insulation, and a double wrap of water-proof material to keep the insulation dry and help prevent a freeze-up during extremely cold weather. The second thaw cable functioned as a backup in case the first burned out. We covered the water line and the sewer system with dry gravel.

My brother Joe and his wife, Norma, and their two children, Jody and Kurt, came to the lodge just as we were getting ready to open the new addition. They also celebrated their twenty-fifth wedding anniversary at the lodge.

My wife and daughter and I were still sleeping in the kitchen store room, so I decided to remodel the old bathrooms and convert one into sleeping quarters for the family. I converted the other one into an office.

First Boat Rental

Customers Mike and Alma Fawcett spent a lot of time at their cabin on Lake Susitna after they retired. Mike was a former pilot, and he was familiar with different types of boats and snowmachines. He also used a generator to supply power to his cabin.

With this kind of experience, Mike and Alma were just the right folks to watch the lodge for us when both of us had to go to Anchorage. Judy and I hadn't had a day off from our lodge business for at least five months. We were putting in at least sixteen hours a day, because in summer we had daylight for approximately twenty out of every twenty-four hours.

The first summer we bought five new boats and outboard motors. Since the lake system was quite large, with approximately one hundred miles of lakeshore, we asked customers to tell us where they were going, and we logged them in on a bulletin board. We figured that if the boats didn't return at a reasonable time, I'd fly around the lakes to locate the customers.

For the first several days the system worked out very well. A few days later a couple of guys rented a boat and told us they were going to fish around Lake Louise. It was about 1 p.m. when they rented the boat, and by 10 p.m. they had not returned. Two possibilities had me worried. They might have stolen my new boat and motor, or they might be in some kind of trouble. I wasn't going to bed until I located the missing customers and boat. Flying around the lake I'd locate them more easily than from a boat, so I took off and flew around Lake Louise till I spotted the two fishermen and our boat.

I landed a short distance away from them, taxied up close, and asked them when they were planning to bring the boat back to the lodge. They told me they'd rented the boat for the day and it was still daylight, so what did I want them to do. We agreed they'd have the boat back by midnight. The very next day we changed our boat rental policy, and rented the boats for eight-hour periods.

Since days were so long during the summer months, we had customers around the lodge at all hours. Some got off work at midnight and drove the 180 miles to the lodge in four or five hours. They arrived at the lodge in daylight and would either use their own boats to go to their cabins, or rent one of ours.

Judy and I worked out a shift schedule. Judy opened the lodge at 6 a.m. in summer, and tried to get to bed by 10:00 or 10:30 p.m. I tried to sleep till 10 a.m. and stayed up till 2 a.m. We did this every day, seven days a week, eleven months a year.

By the second year at the lodge we had a few dollars put aside for a well-deserved vacation. We decided to visit Judy's folks in Orlando, Florida.

Floatplane Landings

I had more than two hundred hours of flying on wheels and skis, but I didn't have any experience with floatplane flying. A friend of mine gave me a couple of tips on taking off and landing a floatplane, but I didn't have any flight instruction on it. I was anxious to get some experience flying my new Super Cub on floats, so every chance I had I went flying.

Although I'd heard a lot about glassy-water landings, I'd never tried it. One of our customers told me he forgot to lock his cabin on Lake Louise, and he would appreciate it if I would check it the next time I went by there in my boat or plane.

The following day was beautiful and calm, and I figured it would be a good time for me to practice glassy-water landing. I told Judy I was going down the lake to check on a customer's cabin, and I'd be back shortly.

The cabin was in a small cove, so I set up my landing approach. Looking at the water was like looking in a mirror. I couldn't tell how high I was off the water. I added power and went around for another approach, figuring that if I couldn't tell how high I was by looking at the lake, I would look at the trees growing next to the lake to get some depth perception.

The idea sounded good in theory, but in real life I cut the power when I thought I was close to the water and the plane dropped like a rock. I was sure I'd split the floats or at least bent the wings on the airplane, but when I checked it over I could find no damage. I checked the cabin, and indeed he'd left it unlocked. After I locked up I decided I needed some lessons in floatplane flying.

Back at the lodge I was glad the wind had put a few small waves on the lake so I didn't have to make another glassy-water landing. I contacted my former flight instructor, Ed Broome, and he gave me a couple of hour's instruction. He also accompanied me to Anchorage to get a check ride for my floatplane rating.

Our pilot was busy flying hunters out for moose and caribou when John, one of his friends, came to visit. John was in the military, and he had recently been transferred to Alaska. He wanted to get a caribou but our pilot was too busy to take him hunting, so I decided to take John out for a hunt. I got him outfitted with a pair of hip boots, and I let him borrow one of my rifles. By the time we found some caribou it was getting late in the day, and after John got one and we processed the animal it was almost dark.

John was also a pilot, and on the flight back to the lodge he asked me if I had ever made a night landing. I told him no, and that got him a bit excited. He leaned forward from the back seat until he was looking right over my shoulder. Had I ever made a glassy-water landing, he wanted to know. I said yes, but it hadn't been very pretty. I thought he was going to jump into the front seat and take over flying the plane. As we neared the lodge I set up an approach for a glassy-water landing. I knew that a point of land in front of the lodge, called Army Point, was quite a distance from the lodge. I made a beautiful landing and John gave me a couple of whacks on the shoulder.

When we got to the docks he said I'd really had him going. He didn't know me that well, and he didn't know how much experience I had doing night landings. When I told him that had really been my first, he didn't know whether to believe me or not.

Drain Field

My neighbor, Bill Poe, told me that my water and sewer systems wouldn't work in winter. The army and air force recreation camps couldn't keep their systems running during the winter months, so who did I think I was anyway?

Both systems worked well through the summer and fall seasons. The first time the temperature dropped to 45 degrees below zero, Bill stopped by and asked, "Well, teach, how well is your new water and sewer system working?" With a smile on my face I said, "They're working just fine, Bill. Go in and flush the john to your heart's content."

A month later that smile on my face turned into a frown. During Christmas vacation we had around forty guests at the lodge, and Judy was using the basement as a place to dry the sheets we used in the cabins. One day when she went down to get some sheets she found about 3 inches of water on the floor. I went down to see if I could find the source of the water, checked my water pump and water line several times, but couldn't find a leak.

When I pumped the basement dry I found the source of the water. It was coming from my leach field through the loose gravel we had backfilled against the basement wall. Lucky for me, Al Gruchow, a friend from the school district, and his family were staying at the lodge. Al and I discussed and cussed the problem and we decided to bypass the leach field to stop the water from going into the basement. We had to dig a trench 3 feet long and several feet deep to get to the outflow of the septic tank. The pick-and-shovel routine didn't work–the ground was frozen solid. No matter how hard we swung the pick, it left only a dent in the ground. Next we tried building a fire on top of the ditch, but we couldn't soften the earth enough to do any good. Al made the 100-mile round trip to Glennallen and returned with an asphalt preheater about 18 inches wide and 3 feet long. The preheater used propane as a source of fuel, so we hooked it up to a 100-pound cylinder of propane. We suspended the heater close to the ground and actually cooked our way through the frozen earth to the depth we needed to bypass the drain field.

To store the liquid coming out of the septic tank we needed a holding tank. Al suggested we use the old trailer Judy and I had stayed in on our first visit to the lodge. We stripped the inside of the trailer of everything except for the oil-burning heater I'd been so concerned about on that visit, cut out the back of the trailer, and slid in a 1,000-gallon old fuel tank to use as a holding tank. I had enough valves and pipefittings to bypass the drain field, and some extra thaw lines and insulation to complete the job.

The bypass system worked great except that I had to keep track of the liquid in the tank to make sure it did not overflow and leak into the lake. I also had to keep tabs on the heater, because if it went out the 1,000-gallon tank of liquid would freeze solid, and we'd be out of business.

Next I rigged up a 500-gallon tank on an old trailer to haul the liquid to the sanitary fill about two miles from the lake. In winter I had to keep the water pump warm with a space heater to keep it from freezing up, and I kept a propane weed burner with me on the trip, since the valve on the 500-gallon tank would freeze shut. I had to heat it to open the valve to drain the liquid. This routine lasted all winter long, but I was determined to have indoor plumbing for my family and for the guests in the lodge.

When summer came I knew I had to dig up all the water and sewer lines. I didn't want to go for a second time through the experience of having to cook through the dirt to dig another wintertime ditch. Nor did I want to risk digging up the 150-foot water line with a backhoe. That could destroy the very expensive thaw lines and the insulation around the pipe, so we dug the long ditch by hand. This time I made the ditch wide enough so I could place logs on both sides of the pipe.

We constructed a wide tunnel for a Utilidor-style power vault so that I would have enough room inside it to work on the line if the pipe broke or if a thaw line burned out. I strung a set of lights in the Utilidor and installed a trap door on both ends. Building the Utilidor was a lot of hard work, but it gave me the satisfaction of knowing that I would have access to the water line any time of year.

Water Line

When ice formed on the lake I had to move the water line out further into the lake, so I drilled several holes in the ice until I found water about 4 feet deep. I extended the water line on top of the ice along with the necessary insulation and thaw cables. The system worked fine all winter long but I knew when the ice started to break up I'd have to design a different system.

No one else around the lakes had a year-round water system, so I had to develop something original. The former owner, Doc Pease, had collected quite a few sections of what looked like a narrow wooden walkway, designed for the military. They were painted an olive drab color. The sections were extremely well built, so I eased each section underneath the insulated water line as a support. The sections interlocked, so I had a pretty solid-looking system. I drilled holes through the ice on both sides of the project from the shore to the end of the water line, and with a sledgehammer drove cut-up sections of galvanized pipe through the holes into the bottom of the lake.

With heavy-duty wire I attached the walkway sections to the galvanized pipe, crosswiring each section. It took me several days to complete the project, but when it was finished it looked pretty sturdy. I hoped that when the ice melted it would leave my water line suspended on the walkway and pilings. The ice started to melt around the edges of the lake, and so far my water line was in good shape. As more of the ice thawed away I was proud of myself for designing the elevated water line. The ice melted yet a little further from shore, and during the night a strong wind came up.

Judy woke me early in the morning and told me something

was wrong with the water line. When I looked out the window I couldn't believe my eyes. All my hard work was turned into a jumbled mess. The water line had buckled, and the super tough military walkway sections were askew. All the pilings I had driven into the lakebed were bent in two different directions.

I was dumbfounded. Evidently the wind had moved the ice toward the lodge and then changed direction. It was hard to believe that wind could move the ice on a lake 8 miles long and 3 miles wide, especially with several islands and bays scattered around.

After I had a good talk with the Lord I went back to bed for a couple more hours. After breakfast I went to work tearing apart and salvaging what I could of my seriously damaged water line. I'd thought I had a good idea with this elevated line, but now it was back to the drawing board.

Hooking up a temporary water line solved the immediate problem, but before another winter came I was going to have to come up with a better plan. I thought of driving more pilings into the lake bed or even installing bigger pilings, but from what I'd seen of the power of the moving ice I figured whatever I invented would have to be very sturdy. The only reasonable idea I could come up with was to join Mother Nature, not fight her. I decided to build a gravel spit out into the lake to support the water line.

I had purchased a small crawler-type bucket loader and a 2-yard dump truck. It took quite a few loads of gravel to build the spit out to a point where I had at least 4 feet of water.

The gravel spit worked well that winter and through the spring break-up. However, during the summer the waves from boats going to and from the docks washed away some of the gravel. To solve this problem, I bought a load of blown-down logs. Larry Sine, one of our customers, helped me beef up the gravel spit with these logs, and again I drove more pilings into the lakebed, but this time it was a lot easier. I used the hydraulics of the bucket loader to pound the pilings into the lake bottom.

The new gravel spit also worked well as an auxiliary dock for visiting boats and airplanes that were on floats. I also used it to tie up portions of the dock when I took the dock apart in October.

Payback

We wanted to do something nice for the friends and teachers who had helped us get the lodge cleaned up. Bill Poe had told me that hardly anyone came to the lake during the holidays, so we contacted all the people who'd helped us clean up and invited them to come to the lodge for a free Thanksgiving holiday. Al Gruchow bought five snowmachines and we worked out an agreement that would allow us to rent the snowmachines as part of the lodge operation.

Judy cooked three turkeys with all the trimmings, and we were looking forward to a very nice holiday with all the people who'd helped us earlier in the year. Quite a few of our friends came to the lodge, and other people were asking if they could join us. We didn't turn anyone away, and Judy had to cook two more hams so that we would have enough food for everyone. After dinner everyone helped clean up and offered to help Judy in the kitchen.

That Thanksgiving dinner started a tradition that helped us to be a success for the seven years that we owned the lodge. Our second Thanksgiving holiday brought even more customers to the lodge, and we were booked solid. The cabins were full and we rented out the couches and the recliners in the lodge. After the couches and recliners were full we rented out spaces on the floor. We furnished these folks with sleeping bags, but quite often they brought their own.

A young family of four came to the lodge one day and asked if they could join us for dinner and stay overnight. We told them they could stay for dinner, but we were completely booked and people were sleeping on the couches and on the floor. The lady looked at the large harvest table we had in the lodge and asked if anyone was scheduled to sleep under it. Since no one had asked about that spot the young family had dinner with us and slept under the table.

During the Christmas holidays we received a call on our high-frequency radio from the same family, asking if they could make a reservation. The lady said she knew we were probably booked, but if no one had reserved the harvest table, they would like to reserve that space. We reserved the space under the table for the family and they joined us for the Christmas holiday.

We ended up with a lot of strange comments in our guest register. One lady wrote that this was the biggest bedroom she had ever slept in. Another lady noted that she had never slept with so many men in her life.

A few times customers walked out of the lodge without paying for a meal. They'd return and apologize, and they explained that they'd forgotten to pay because it was just like going to grandma's house for the holidays. We told them that was the best compliment they could give us.

Central Alaska Missions

Our daughter, AnnMarie, had turned three years old shortly after we purchased the lodge. We had a nice birthday party for her and the summer help treated her like their little sister. She enjoyed having tea parties with the summer workers, and with some of the kids who came to the lodge with their parents.

The addition to the lodge had several large thermopane windows facing the lake, and quite often birds would hit a window and break their necks. AnnMarie always had a soft spot for any type of bird or animal. When she found a dead bird she'd wrap it up in newspaper and give it to me to send to God. I'd take the package and place it on top of the lodge roof. This seemed to satisfy her, and, of course, I had to remember to dispose of the dead bird before the cat found it.

The Central Alaska Missions in Glennallen owned a small building close to our lodge, and during the summer months they conducted Sunday School classes. We allowed our daughter to attend those classes, and one day when she came home we asked her what she had learned. She said they'd learned all about Jesus Crust. We asked if they had talked about Jesus Christ, but she said no, she was quite sure it was Jesus Crust.

The Central Alaska Missions owned the hospital and the radio station in Glennallen, and the radio station offered a message service to people in the remote areas, or as most Alaskans call it, "the bush." Since there were no telephones in these areas and very few high-frequency radios, the message service called "Caribou Clatter" was an important link to the outside world.

Before we installed the high-frequency radio and hooked up with an answering service in Anchorage, the only communication we had was a citizens band radio, which had a limited range of perhaps five miles if the conditions were right. In order for our customers to make a reservation at the lodge they'd have to call the Glennallen radio station and ask if they would send a Caribou Clatter to Barney and Judy at Evergreen Lodge at Lake Louise. Station personnel took the information and twice a day they broadcast the messages.

Every day we turned to KCAM, the Glennallen station, to check if we had any messages. They usually said something like, "Please reserve a cabin for four people for the Taylor family. We will be there by dinnertime. Please turn on the heat so the cabin will be warm when we arrive." This radio station provided an important link for the people living in the bush, for they depended on their ability to receive messages from the outside world, and on access to the latest weather reports.

Our daughter AnnMarie

AnnMarie

One weekend a family came to the lodge with a daughter who played the guitar. She could really play, and she sang quite a few songs for our customers.

After the guests left, our daughter, who was around three years old at the time, found an old guitar that had been left at the lodge. It had only two strings on it, and it was pretty beat up, but she started plunking on the strings and sang us a song. The song went on for quite a while about the lodge, the cat, the dog, the trees, and anything else that came to her mind.

When she was old enough to start kindergarten, we signed her up for a correspondence course that was offered by the State of Alaska. In the box they sent us was everything necessary for teaching kindergarten. Judy set aside a couple of hours when she was not busy with lodge activities to teach our daughter.

Since a lot of customers were teachers, they often brought study materials as supplements to the materials provided by the State. When we closed the lodge in October we took AnnMarie to Hawaii or Mexico and she'd report on these areas as part of her class work. By the time we sold the lodge she had completed fourth grade by home study.

As AnnMarie got a bit older she proved to be a good helper for Judy in the kitchen, and making up beds in the cabins. She also helped me when I made repairs on a snowmachine or on my bucket loader. I taught her different sizes of wrenches, and the names of various other tools. While I was under the loader or other equipment she acted as my gofer, bringing me a wrench or a socket so that I didn't have to keep rolling out from underneath.

She liked to go to the sanitary fill with me, because I let her sit in my lap so she could steer the truck down the road. We also took the .22 rifle with us, and practiced shooting at bottles and cans. She enjoyed riding and driving the snowmachines we had for rent. As she got a little older, her job was to sweep the snow off the machines, and she got to drive them down to the gas pumps to get in a little more driving time. Judy had experience teaching skiing to little kids in Yosemite National Park, and she taught AnnMarie to ski on the hill adjacent to the lodge.

One year during the Christmas vacation we had quite a few British Petroleum employees at the lodge. They brought their children with them, and a number of them were about AnnMarie's age. Some had never seen a frozen lake or played in the snow. Judy helped AnnMarie set up a tea party in the corner of the lodge and gave all the kids snacks. The kids had a good time, and since most were from England, AnnMarie got quite a kick out of the different names they had for the snacks. The English children called pretzels *twiggies* and cookies *sweets*. AnnMarie held up a peanut and asked what it was called. Peanut, they said. She was very pleased that they called a peanut the same thing she called it.

We moved back to Anchorage after we sold the lodge and enrolled AnnMarie in the fifth grade. At our first parent-teacher conference the teacher told us our daughter was well ahead of her classmates in her studies, but did not express herself like a child. She talked freely with teachers and other adults, but was not interested in the chitchat of her classmates.

When we told the teacher that we had owned a remote hunting and fishing lodge catering to people from all around the world, and that AnnMarie had traveled with us to Mexico, Hawaii, and to the British West Indies, he seemed to develop a better understanding of why AnnMarie was so comfortable with adults.

Story Teller

I drove out to the highway to make a phone call to Anchorage to hire a new pilot. I called several pilots I knew, and they recommended Al Burnett. Al agreed to fly up to the lodge for an interview. After I finished my phone call a young man at the bar introduced himself as Rick. He said he didn't mean to listen in on my conversation, but he couldn't help hearing I was looking for a pilot, and maybe he could help me. He was a pilot. We talked a little more and he told me he had owned a Cessna 180 back on the East Coast, but he'd buzzed the beach once too often and the FAA had suspended his license. When he told me he had around five hundred hours of flying time I asked him to stop by the lodge as soon as possible, because I would like to talk to him.

Al Burnett flew up to the lodge, and after an extensive interview he agreed to fly for us. A couple of weeks later, Rick and his wife, Joan, came to the lodge and asked if we needed any help. Judy and I decided to hire Rick as a handyman and Joan as a helper in the kitchen. A few days later Rick remarked that his wife and I had a lot in common. He understood that I was a former school administrator and his wife had worked as an executive for a large corporation and made multimillion-dollar decisions. When I mentioned something to Joan about her employment as an executive, she didn't know what I was talking about. I told her what her husband had said about her big-money decisions, and she told me she had worked for a large corporation, as a custodian.

We were so busy at the lodge that Judy and I didn't have much time to compare notes about our new employees, When we were sitting by the fireplace a few weeks later, Rick asked me if I'd been in the service. I replied that I'd spent three years in the army security agency. He wanted to know if I'd had any exciting experiences in the service. At times it was exciting, I told him, but these were things I couldn't talk about. In answer to my question he revealed that he'd been in the UDT (underwater demolition team), so I invited him to tell me about his exciting experiences.

He warmed right up to that, and told me that when he was in Korea he'd been part of a team of demolition experts assigned the task of blowing up a bridge crossing a certain river. Just about the time they were getting close to bridge a Korean frogman appeared in the water close to him. When Rick pulled out his knife and started swimming for the enemy frogman, the man just swam away from him.

A few days later Rick related this story to one of our customers. The customer was interested because he had served in the same area. When Rick told him the name of the river the customer laughed and said that was hard to believe. That river was so narrow and so shallow that it would have been impossible for anyone to swim in it.

I designed a cabin I wanted to build in a remote, popular hunting area for use by our hunters, and also as a place for our pilots to go to in case they encountered bad weather. Rick helped me precut the lumber for the cabin and build the foundation. We framed up part of the cabin and Rick said he could finish it.

I told our pilot Rick had owned a Cessna 180 and had around five hundred hours of flying time. Since the pilot had an instructor's rating, I asked him to check Rick out on the 180. After a few trips to the cabin site I asked our pilot/instructor how Rick was doing with his flying lessons and he asked me again how many flying hours Rick had. When I told him about five hundred he just laughed. Rick did not know where the throttle was on the 180.

Rick and Joan were good employees, but Rick's stories got to the point that no one believed anything he said. The busy hunting season came to an end and Rick and Joan decided to seek employment in another area.

Fish and Game Officers

During the hunting season we got a lot of visits from the fish and game officer in Glennallen. Terry was one of the fish and game officers who came to visit the lodge. He wore his official uniform and on his hip he wore a big pistol. He was always accompanied by his German shepherd dog. Terry also wore his badge of authority as a chip on his shoulder. He was not a pleasant person to deal with.

As our pilots and other private pilots brought in their caribou, Terry would be down by the runway with his dog, to confront them and ask to see their hunting licenses and make sure the hunters had tagged their caribou. A lot of the pilots were hunting caribou for their own meat supply and at times they took a friend out hunting.

On several occasions I talked to Terry about his attitude, and tried to tell him he would get a lot more cooperation out of these pilots if he used a more subtle approach. We also complained to Terry's supervisor about his attitude, and he said he was aware of the problem. A few months later Terry had to go in for a minor operation and when he came back to the lodge we could not believe the difference in his attitude.

Terry sat down, had a cup of tea and a piece of pie–which he had never done before–and started talking to our customers and to some of the pilots. After a few more visits the pilots started to tell him about game violations they had observed, and offered to fly Terry out to observe them for himself.

Terry was transferred to another area, and we got a new officer by the name of Charlie. Charlie seemed to enjoy life; he talked to customers and pilots. It didn't take long for Charlie to learn about the fish and game violations taking place in our area.

Several customers complained about people setting out fishing lines attached to plastic jugs. Sometimes the jugs were hard to see in rough water conditions, and when the boats ran over them the heavy-duty line tied to the jugs wound around their boats' propellers.

One day while Charlie was at the lodge a customer complained to him about the jugs. He used the map we had at the lodge to point out the problem area. Charlie made arrangements with us to have our pilot fly him to the area so he could check out what was going on.

Bill was our pilot at the time, and told us about the incident. He'd flown Charlie to the problem area, and they spotted several plastic jugs floating on the lake so Bill landed the floatplane close by. Charlie got out on the float, and as Bill taxied up to the jugs he grabbed one and started to wind up the heavy-duty line attached to it.

A couple of kids on the beach nearby saw what was happening and started yelling at Charlie. They told him their father had put out the set lines, and was going to be real mad at Charlie for stealing his lines. As Bill taxied up to the next set line, Charlie picked up the second jug and started winding up the line.

Now the mother of the kids came running out of the cabin, and she directed quite a string of profanity at Charlie for picking up her husband's set lines. Charlie told Bill to taxi up to the shoreline. The lady was about to do battle with Charlie when he stepped off the float.

Charlie introduced himself as a fish and game officer, and she did a complete turnaround. She didn't know a thing about the set lines or jug fishing. Charlie gave her a warning and explained to her that jug fishing was illegal. The lady thanked him and took her kids back to the cabin. Word spread around the lakes real quick and we didn't see any more jug fishing the rest of the summer.

Wild Bill

During the summer months hauling trash to the sanitary fill was no great task. All in all it took probably about twenty minutes to a half-hour to complete the job. In winter it took an hour or more just to heat the engine of the vehicle to get it started. Depending on the temperature, sometimes I had to heat the transmission and the differential to get the vehicle to move. This was the part that worried me the most about living in such extreme weather conditions. In case of an accident or illness it would take quite a while to preheat the vehicle to take anyone to the hospital fifty road miles away.

I was determined that by next winter I would have some kind of garage to park my truck in, to keep it warm for just such emergencies. I also needed a place to work on the snowmachines we rented out. It is very difficult to work on any equipment with gloves on, so I'd remove my gloves and work on the machines with my bare hands. It didn't take long to get frostbitten fingers, and it takes quite a while for the fingers to heal. If you have ever touched a hot stove with your fingers you know what frostbitten fingers feel like. Frostbite causes water blisters similar to those of a burn.

One summer day a guy walked into the lodge, asked to speak to the owner, and introduced himself as Bill Nelson. He was putting in a bid to clean up and move quite a few trailers and buildings from the abandoned army and air force recreation sites on Lake Louise. When he mentioned moving buildings he really got my attention, because I knew of two buildings on these sites that I could put to good use.

Bill and I worked out a deal. We would furnish him room and board for his crew and he would do some excavation work around the lodge and allow me to salvage a fairly large building I wanted to use as a workshop, and another smaller building I could use to house my two generators.

Bill turned out to be quite a character, and after a while we found out why he was nicknamed Wild Bill. He told us a few stories about flying his Super Cub. He liked to fly low and buzz his friends' homes. One day he was going to give his neighbor a buzz job and he flew so low he wiped out his neighbors' mailbox and did quite a bit of damage to his airplane.

Bill proved to be a very hard worker and he put in long hours jacking up the trailers and refitting them with axles and wheels. He had to wait until the lake froze solid before he was able to move the trailers and the buildings. The large building I wanted was mounted on skids, so Bill dragged it with his Caterpillar for about 3 miles from the old air force recreation site to the lodge property. By the time Bill got the building onto our property it looked pretty wobbly, but I knew I could convert it into a warm workshop.

I helped Wild Bill jack up the smaller building and we backed a lowboy trailer under it. By the time we were ready to move the building the weather had warmed up considerably, and the ice had started to melt. Still, I didn't think we'd have a problem towing the trailer with the building for about 3 miles across the ice, so I started out across the lake and in about a mile or so I noticed that the ice was starting to look wavy. I knew that if I stopped I would lose my truck along with Wild Bill's trailer and my newly acquired building. I said a quick prayer to the dear Lord, and stepped on the gas pedal. I made it across the lake to the lodge, but I will remember that trip for quite a while.

I converted the large building into a heated shop and installed a set of double doors so that we could put the nose of an airplane into the shop. Then I modified the smaller building to accommodate the 20 KW generator and a 10 KW backup generator. On this building I installed two sets of doors so that I could regulate the temperature. In the summer months I opened all the doors to keep the generator cool, and in winter I kept the generators warm by keeping all the doors closed. This proved to be fruitful, because quite often the 20 KW generator broke down at 65 degrees below zero. Since the heat from the 20 KW kept the 10 KW generator warm, I didn't have any problem starting the 10 KW. The backup generator produced enough power to keep the lights burning in the lodge and cabins, and to keep the heat cables warm on the incoming water line and the sewage system. Without a water supply and a sewage disposal system we would be out of business.

As part of my agreement with Wild Bill he'd agreed to do some excavation work around the lodge. The parking lot consisted of several levels, so I asked Bill to level out the parking lot and haul the excess gravel down to the lake so that I could use it to build a decent boat ramp.

As Wild Bill hauled the gravel down to the lake, I used my bucket loader to push the gravel into the lake to make a ramp we could use to launch and take out the larger boats customers were bringing. When I finished the ramp I raised the fee for launching and taking out a boat from one to two dollars.

The day I put up the new sign for the two-dollar launching fee a man and his wife brought their boat to the lake to go fishing. He saw the new sign and said the fee was outrageous, and he refused to pay it. The dock boys told him I had put a lot of work and money into building the new ramp, but he didn't want to hear anything about it. He told them he could launch his boat at the public campground for free, and he left.

A couple of hours later his wife came walking back to the lodge and asked me if I would go over to the campground and pull their car out of the lake. She said the stubborn old fart had just about ruined their car because he was too cheap to pay the two-dollar fee.

I gave her a ride to the campground in my four-wheel-drive pickup truck, and I took a length of chain with me. The ramp at the campground was not only shallow, but it had quite a few good-sized rocks covered by the water. The guy must have been determined to launch his boat, because he'd backed his vehicle so far into the lake that the water was over the back seat.

I hooked the chain to the man's car and asked him to see if it would help if he also tried driving his car while I was trying to pull him out with my pickup. We tried several times, but I couldn't pull him out of the lake.

By this time he was so angry he wouldn't talk to me. I told his wife that if she wanted me to do it, I'd go back to the lodge and get my bucket loader, and quoted her $40 per hour for my time and the use of the bucket loader. She conferred with her husband and he agreed to the price. With the bucket loader I was able to get enough traction to pull the car and the boat out of the lake. She paid me the $40 and her husband kept busy cleaning up the car.

Tall Nancy

One day during the summer a customer remarked how well we had planned our family. Judy asked what she meant, and she said it must have taken quite a bit of planning on our part to have the children spaced so well that we had one son old enough to fly the airplanes, a daughter old enough to work in the kitchen, and two more boys old enough to help on the docks. Judy told her that David Goocey, our pilot, was not our son and Nancy, who worked in the kitchen, was not our daughter. Furthermore, the two dock boys were not related to us, either. We had only one daughter, Judy explained, and she was only three years old.

Judy and I had often mentioned how unusual it was that the summer help always looked like they all came from the same family. One summer all the help would have brown hair, and another summer they'd be redheads or blondes. Some were high school students and others were in college. A lot came from Alaska, and others came from various parts of the United States.

One summer a young couple came to the lodge and during lunch they mentioned that they were on their way to Fairbanks to attend the University of Alaska. Nancy was a tall girl, around six feet, and very attractive. They asked if we could use some help for a few weeks until they had to go back to college. Judy put Nancy to work helping her in the kitchen, and Nancy's friend helped me with a few projects around the lodge. Nancy seemed to become part of our family and she enjoyed having tea parties with AnnMarie.

Tall Nancy and her friend returned to college, and since she got along so well with us we began to act as her adopted parents.

She came to the lodge to help out for the holidays, and when she brought a friend along she asked us to observe him. Before she left she always asked our opinion of the friend.

One Thanksgiving holiday tall Nancy came to help and brought a friend. I had a chance to visit with him, and he told me he was related to the deBeers, the diamond family. When I asked him why he didn't use the name, he said he was the black sheep of the family and they didn't want anything to do with him. He'd been in a lot of trouble and had been given the choice of going to jail or joining the French Foreign Legion. He'd joined the Legion and stayed with them for several years. After he left he had enough money to go into business for himself. He liked foreign sports cars, so he decided to go into the business of repairing such cars. He'd been very successful in setting up this type of repair shop in various parts of the country, and had decided to go to Fairbanks because he'd heard about the big money that was being made on the Alaska pipeline project. In answer to my question why he was so successful, he said he always paid top dollar to all his mechanics, and therefore he always got the best mechanics available in the area.

We talked a little more, and when he found out I was a pilot he wanted me to fly him to Mexico to look at a piece of property he wanted to develop into a first-class resort. I told him we'd been to Mexico, and if I remembered correctly, an American could not own beachfront property. He said that quite a few years ago his relatives, the deBeers family, had done a big favor for the president of Mexico, and in return he had given them a huge piece of water-front property.

A few weeks later tall Nancy returned to the lodge with her boyfriend and they were talking about getting married. Again Nancy asked us to talk to him and check him out. While I was talking with him he asked me about the island we owned in the middle of Lake Louise. He'd like to use a snowmachine to take Nancy out to look at the island. After they returned he told me that since the island was such a beautiful piece of property he would like to buy it for Nancy as a wedding gift.

We agreed on a price and I called our attorney, Brian Brundin, to draw up the necessary papers. Nancy's friend gave me a check for $10,000 as a down payment and said he would pay me the balance on closing.

The check was returned for insufficient funds. I called Nancy's friend and he told me his secretary had fouled up and put his deposit in the wrong account. We deposited the check again and it was returned again. Insufficient funds. I called the friend back and he told me he was having some trouble with his business because his manager had taken off with some of his money. After that I called Nancy and told her what was going on. She said she'd check into it and call us back. A few days later she called. She could not locate her friend, or her car.

A short time later she came to the lodge and told us her friend was a phony. He didn't have the money to buy the island, and he'd tried to steal her car. When Nancy talked to the police about him she found out they had a warrant out for his arrest. Evidently, he was quite a con man and was wanted in one or more states for similar activities. We now call Nancy's former friend the "count no count."

Big Fish

In the summer of 1971 Judy's brother, John, had to have a cornea transplant. His wife, Donna, wrote and asked if we could take care of their two kids–Kristine, who was fourteen, and John, age eleven–for the summer while John recuperated. We agreed to take care of the youngsters and picked them up in Anchorage after their school was out in June. Kris helped Judy in the kitchen and she also helped clean up cabins and do laundry.

Kris and John were well-behaved kids, so we took them salmon fishing on the Gulkana River. Kris and John's dad owned a charter boat service in Port Angeles, Washington, so both knew quite a bit about salmon fishing from a boat, but they had never been salmon fishing on a river.

A customer had told us how to find a trail that would take us to a good fishing spot on the Gulkana River. Judy and I had fished this spot before and when the fish were running it was a tremendous fishing experience. We took our pilot with us to give him a break from flying, and drove to Glennallen. It was quite a hike to the fishing hole, but everyone made it without any problem.

We'd taken our best fishing poles and some heavy-duty fishing reels. Kris hooked a nice, big king salmon and fought it for quite a while. Finally she got the big fish to the edge of the river, and our pilot tried to help her get it on the bank. Just as he touched the fish it gathered enough power to straighten out the hooks and it swam away. Kris was tired and disappointed, but she knew from fishing with her father that you don't always get to keep the fish you hook.

A little while later I hooked a big king, and it put up such a battle in the swift water that my fishing pole broke. The fish stayed on the line, but I had a hard time trying to reel it in with the broken pole.

The salmon stopped running, so our pilot brought his fishing pole over to me. We decided to try cutting my line and retying it to his fishing line. I wrapped some of my fishing line around my hand and Judy and the pilot cut my line and tied it to his. I had some difficulty working the knot through the guides on the fishing poles, but once I got it past the smaller guides I was able to land the fish.

The weather on the Fourth of July weekend was beautiful, and we were super busy. Kitty and Dale Belmonte were helping us part time so that Judy and I could get some sleep. It seemed like we had just fallen asleep when Kris woke us up to take a picture of a big lake trout. Judy told Kris the bulletin board was full of pictures of big fish and she would take a picture after we got a few more hours of sleep.

Kris insisted that the fish was really huge and the fisherman wanted us to take a picture of his trophy. Finally, Judy gave in and got dressed, and went outside to take a picture of this big fish. A few minutes later she woke me up and asked me to come and take a look at the trophy lake trout.

The fish was amazing. In answer to my question the fisherman said he was definitely going to have it mounted because it was the biggest fish he'd ever caught. I measured it at 42 inches in length, and it tipped the scales at 44 pounds. I put it in the freezer and we went inside to have a cup of coffee.

The fisherman told us he'd been fishing out of his canoe by the outlet of Lake Louise very early in the morning. The fish hit his lure so hard it almost tore the fishing rod out of his hand, then started towing the canoe around the lake with the fisherman and his young dog on board.

This went on for about forty-five minutes, and he said he was getting scared, thinking perhaps that he'd hooked into the Lake Louise monster if there was such a thing. He thought of hollering for help, but it was the Fourth of July weekend, and people would think he was drunk, and ignore him.

Eventually, the fish got tired and he was able to reel it close to his canoe. When he got a good look at the trout he couldn't believe his eyes. Since he had no net with him, he just scooped up the fish with his hands and threw it into the canoe. That got his young dog excited and he almost tipped them over.

He knew he had a big one, so he paddled as fast as he could back to the lodge—an eight-mile trip. Everyone around the lodge congratulated him and he left to drive back to Anchorage.

A few weeks later we saw him in Anchorage and I asked him if he'd had his fish mounted. He told me he wasn't able to afford it just yet, because when he got home after this fishing trip he'd found a big note on the door from his wife, which read, "I hate your guts, you SOB, and I filed for divorce."

Judy and I both said we were sorry, but he told us he was happy. He'd caught a trophy fish and got rid of his wife, too.

My Pet Elephant

During our first year at the lodge I had to do everything by hand. When a hole in the road or in the parking lot needed patching, I had to shovel gravel into my pickup truck, and shovel and spread it by hand. When a section of the dock had to be moved, I had to wait until enough guys showed up to help me. When it snowed quite a bit I had to use the four-wheel-drive truck to pack down the snow on the road leading to the lodge.

The following spring I saw an ad in the Anchorage newspaper listing a small crawler-type bucket loader for sale. I purchased the loader and it turned out to be my pet elephant. Al Gruchow let me borrow a small dump truck. I thought I was in heaven. I could load gravel with the bucket loader, dump it without having to lift a shovel, and spread it with the loader. The pet elephant helped with my sore-back problems and cut down on the blisters on my hands.

I designed a completely new dock system and as I built the dock sections I could move them around with the loader. The loader also came in handy when I was installing the dock in the summer and removing it in October.

A lot of our customers brought the trash from their cabin sites and left it in our trash barrels by the docks. As we got more customers to keep their boats on our dock, the trash I hauled to the landfill had grown to a sizable amount. The landfill was several miles from the lodge, but no one maintained it.

Since we were in the Matanuska Borough I contacted the Borough and told them the trash problem was getting out of hand.

Since no one else in the area had any excavating equipment, I worked out a contract with the Borough to maintain the sanitary fill. In the summer I excavated several large trenches and as they filled up with trash I covered them with dirt. Before the ground froze in the fall I excavated several more trenches and during winter I covered the trash with snow. When the ground thawed I covered the winter trash with dirt.

When the army and air force had their recreation camps on Lake Louise, they also maintained the Lake Louise airstrip, but by the time we purchased the lodge, the military camps had been abandoned and no one maintained it.

I contacted the Alaska Division of Aviation and through Jim Amos, who worked for them at the time, I worked out a contract to maintain the airstrip. It was approximately 5,000 feet long, and after I started to maintain it a lot of pilots used it in the summer months because there was no place else to land a plane on wheels except the gravel road. When a vehicle was present, road takeoffs and landings could be hazardous to your health.

I installed a couple of cable tie-downs for aircraft and also put up a windsock and an outhouse. We told our customers that the airstrip was available, and that if they wanted us to pick them up at the airstrip, all they had to do was buzz the lodge a couple of times and we'd drive over to get them.

Judy had worked in Yosemite National Park as a nurse, as had Ginny, a good friend of hers. Ginny had moved to Hawaii and we'd visited with her there, and invited her to visit us at the lodge. We received a letter from Ginny saying she'd made reservations to travel to Alaska and she'd like to visit us.

Ginny liked adventure, so when we told her that her options were to fly to Anchorage and have us pick her up there, and chartering a flight to Lake Louise, she chose to charter the small-airplane flight. Judy told her about the system of buzzing the lodge to signal that she needed to be picked up.

It was a beautiful day when Ginny chartered a plane to Lake Louise, which is only about an hour's flight from Anchorage. This flight is an eye opener. The route goes over the Matanuska Valley, past Matanuska Glacier, and past Sheep Mountain. The pilot knew about Evergreen Lodge, so he had no problem finding it. He buzzed the lodge a couple of times, and since Judy and I were expecting Ginny's arrival, we both drove to the airstrip to pick her up. When we got there, the pilot had already taken off and left Ginny standing there in her Hawaiian dress, her suitcase beside her.

After a couple of hugs she said she didn't know what she would have done if we hadn't picked her up. She figured she was flying to a small airport with a terminal and someone she could talk to about arranging transportation to our lodge. I don't know what she would have done if a big moose or grizzly bear had walked out on the airstrip.

Ginny stayed for a week, and she had a chance to meet a lot of our customers. She enjoyed staying in a log cabin and she and Judy had some time to talk about their different experiences.

A few months later Judy received a letter from Jan Schlintz, a mutual friend of hers and Ginny's. Jan was going through a divorce. We talked about it, and Judy invited her friend to come to the lodge for a visit. Jan accepted the offer and she helped Judy around the lodge for a month or so. Then she returned home to California.

Earlier that summer Judy's brother, Ward, and Kurt had driven our new four-wheel-drive truck from Merced, California, to the lodge. My brother Joe was able to buy the truck for us at a sizable discount, so that helped pay the cost of driving the vehicle to Alaska and the return airfare.

My niece, Barbara Ann Jyachosky, was able to visit with us. I took her fishing on Lake Louise and we were able to show her some of the interesting places around Anchorage. My cousin, Dr. Cibrick, and his wife, Margaret, came to stay with us for a week. I took him fishing and also arranged for him and his wife to fly out with Al Lee, a local guide, to do some salmon fishing.

Judy's sister, Ann Masterson, had moved to Anchorage with her family, so we were able to visit with them quite a few times. Judy's sister Jane came to visit us when their parents were also at the lodge. It was nice to visit with the various relatives, since they were able to keep us informed on what was going on in everyday life.

Stranded

The first year we owned the lodge we closed for the month of October. After we pulled the docks out of the water and put the outboard motors in storage, I had some time to do a little exploring around the area. I wanted to find a remote lake where I could build a cabin we could use for our hunters and fishermen. After flying around for quite a while I found a lake close to a good hunting area, and it looked like a suitable place to build a cabin.

On my way back to the lodge I spotted a Cessna 180 on a very small lake. As I circled, two guys started waving and motioning for me to land. I decided not to land on that small lake, but landed on a larger adjacent one. I tied up my Super Cub and walked over to talk with the guys. The pilot had landed on the lake but misjudged its size, and he could not get up enough airspeed to take off.

I asked if he had tried lightening his load by draining off some of his fuel supply and trying takeoff without his passenger. He said he'd tried that, but it didn't work. He didn't know what else to do except call for a helicopter to lift the plane to an adjacent lake.

It was only a short distance across the brush to the larger lake, so I asked if he had a saw or hatchet with him. He didn't have either, so I went back to my Super Cub and brought back a small saw I carried with my survival gear.

I had an idea that might work–cut a bunch of small trees into 2-foot lengths to make a path from the small lake to the bigger lake where I was parked. Both guys looked at me like I was nuts, but they were willing to try anything.

We cut up quite a few of the small trees that were two to three inches in diameter, and made two paths between the lakes. After all the small logs were in place, I asked the pilot to taxi the 180 up to the path of logs, and his partner to take hold of the wing struts on one side of the plane while I grabbed those on the other side.

Next I told the pilot and his partner that a whistle from me would be the signal to add power to the plane and push on the struts, and we'd try to guide the plane across the small logs to the bigger lake. I whistled and the pilot added power, and with a lot of pushing on our part the pilot got the skeg of the floats on the logs. From there it was a fairly easy job to guide the plane across the logs.

The two men thanked me very much, and when I asked the pilot his name he was reluctant to tell me. He said he was of Polish descent and was afraid I'd make fun of him. I told him I was of Slavic descent and I'd heard my share of Polish jokes, so I knew what he was talking about. Both of us flew back to the lodge and we had a cup of coffee and a piece of Judy's homemade pie. We parted as friends, but that was the last time I saw him.

Incidents

One year the Fish and Game Department opened the hunting season for caribou from August until the end of March. The caribou numbered in the thousands, and combined with a relatively mild winter–for Alaska–those numbers added up to perfect conditions for a lot of pilots and hunters to stock up their freezers with venison.

At times in the winter we had eight or more airplanes parked along the side of the runway. Most of the pilots and their passengers were hunting caribou, and a few came to the lodge to do some ice fishing for lake trout or lingcod.

Larry Thompson was one of our regular weekend customers. He was an avid hunter and a very good pilot. Once Larry flew one of his friends out to hunt caribou and when he didn't return in a reasonable amount of time, we became concerned. We mentioned this to Al Burnett and Dave Goocey, who were flying for us at the time.

Al knew where Larry was hunting, so on his next trip he took the extra time to look for him. He spotted Larry and landed on the same lake to see if he could give him a hand. Larry had bent the propeller on his airplane on landing and he could not take off.

Al flew Larry back to the lodge and Larry called a friend of his in Anchorage on our high-frequency radio, and asked him to bring a new propeller to the lodge. When he related how he bent the propeller, his friend had a good laugh, but he flew up to the lodge with a new propeller. Both flew out to install the new prop on Larry's plane. It worked fine and they flew back. Larry's friend decided that since he was in the area, he wanted to hunt for some caribou. When he didn't return in a reasonable amount of time, Larry flew out to look for him. He found his friend on another lake, and the friend had bent the propeller on his airplane when he landed. I guess the moral of this episode is that "he who laughs last, laughs best."

Lieutenant Colonel Lappo was also one of our regular customers, and a pilot with a lot of flying time to his credit. He also liked to fly some of his friends out to go caribou hunting. One day he returned to the lodge after a short while, and instead of landing on the runway he buzzed the lodge several times. We went outside to see what was going on, and saw that he had something strapped to one of his skis.

We cleared the runway of planes and vehicles, and when he saw what we were doing he continued to circle the area. When all the vehicles and aircraft were cleared, he set up a long and slow approach and did an excellent job of landing on one ski. When the second ski touched down he was able to keep the airplane on the runway.

After he taxied to a stop we saw what he had strapped to the ski. He had broken the ski on landing, and knew he could not take off with a broken ski, so he'd cut down a small tree and used it as a brace. He'd tied the log onto the ski, and made his way back to the lodge.

Larry Thompson knew that we were looking around for a good Cessna 180 to buy, so he flew a 180 up to the lodge for me to look over. Larry was in the aircraft repair business, and he knew a lot about airplanes. The 180 he brought up was a really nice-looking aircraft with low hours on the engine. Larry took me for a demonstration flight, and I was impressed.

After the demonstration flight Larry dropped me off at the lodge and flew out to do some hunting. When he returned a little later he was flying with another pilot. From what he told me, he'd spotted some caribou on a small lake, and when he landed he had too much speed and ended up putting the 180 up into some small trees. He got some his friends to help him retrieve the 180, and was able to fly it back to Anchorage.

A similar incident happened to a teacher friend of ours. When he landed his 180 on a small lake he also came in too fast and his airplane ended up in the brush. The pilot and two of his friends spent the night out in the boonies, but they were fortunate to have their survival gear with them. Dave Goocey spotted them the following day and flew them back to the lodge. The plane was not seriously damaged; he was able to patch it up with Super Cub tape (duct tape) and flew it back to Anchorage.

Doc, one of our dentist friends, flew up to the lodge in his Cessna 180 during the fall hunting season. Later that day he and his friends spotted some caribou by the Susitna River. He landed his 180 on the river and they shot a couple of the animals. It was getting late in the day, and Doc knew he had to hurry up to make it back to the lodge before dark. He told me that as they were finishing up processing the caribou he got a bit careless, and the knife he was using slipped and put a deep cut into his thigh. He had the presence of mind to put a tourniquet on it to stop the bleeding.

Doc was the only one in his party who knew how to fly the 180, so they got into the airplane as fast as they could and Doc flew the plane back to the lodge. When he hobbled inside he explained how he'd injured himself. I don't like to see blood on any human being but since Judy was busy cooking I told Doc I would take a look at the injury and see what I could do for him.

In the bathroom he dropped his pants and sat down on the stool. When he loosened the tourniquet the blood rushed out of his wound. I knew this was more than I could handle so I called Judy. Being a nurse, she knew the wound was serious and he needed immediate medical attention. I let Doc and his friends borrow my truck and they drove him up to the Glennallen hospital. A few hours later they returned to the lodge and told us the doctors in Glennallen were able to repair the damage Doc had done to his leg.

Cessna 180 on floats

Navion

Judy had to make a trip to Anchorage for a doctor's appointment, and Al Burnett had to take care of some business in Anchorage. Judy was not fond of flying but she decided to fly with Al rather than drive the 360-mile round trip. Larry Thompson had flown his low-wing Navion up to the lake and offered to let Al fly the Navion to Anchorage, because it was faster than the Cessna 180 Al was flying. Al had not flown a Navion for quite a while and wanted to make sure he remembered how, so he did the necessary three takeoffs and landings to familiarize himself with the aircraft.

Judy reluctantly got into the Navion and they set out on their one-hour flight to Anchorage. As they approached Merrill Field Al contacted the tower for landing instructions and started the final approach. The tower called him on the radio and told him the landing gear was still in the *up* position. Al tried to lower the landing gear, but it wouldn't go down, so the tower advised him to go around and try the approach again. Al circled the field and made another attempt to lower the gear, but again it did not work. Judy was starting to get nervous about the whole idea, especially since Al had to make a third trip around the field. He tried to manually pump the gear into the *down* position but it was no use.

Al told the tower the gear wouldn't go down even when he tried to do it manually. The tower acknowledged the problem and told him they would foam the runway so that he could land with the gear in the *up* position. By this time Judy was almost in a sheer panic and grabbed Al's leg so hard she could feel the pain in her hand.

Al requested permission to make one more landing attempt, and as he dropped the nose of the Navion the gear started to lower and he was able to make a successful landing. Evidently, the Navion was designed so that if the plane had a nose-high attitude the gear would not go down. When Al taxied over to the tie-down spot Judy said she could hardly get out of the airplane. Her knees were still shaking when she tried to walk away.

A couple of hours later Judy and Al met at the airplane for their flight back to the lodge. The trip went smoothly, but it was dark when they approached the runway. I had gone out to the highway to check the mail and hadn't returned when Al buzzed the lodge. The people we had working for us at that time figured that the plane wanted to land but perhaps the pilot couldn't see the runway. They started up two snowmachines and drove them down to the runway, parking one snowmachine on either side with the lights pointing toward the incoming airplane. The employees had good intentions but the lights took away Al's night vision so that he was unable to see the runway.

Al made a couple more passes over the runway and the employees moved the snowmachines away. He landed safely, but by that time Judy was almost a total wreck. I took quite a while before she decided to go flying again.

During the second moose season Al spotted a moose with a huge rack that would probably measure around 70 inches, Since I had already shot a trophy moose, I wanted Judy to have a chance to get one.

Judy was busy in the kitchen, but when we told her about the trophy moose she decided she'd go flying again. She got dressed in her warm boots and her insulated jumpsuit, and the three of us got into the Cessna 180. Al flew us to the area where he'd spotted the moose, and when we saw him we agreed he would be a nice trophy.

Al landed the plane on a small lake nearby and we carefully walked up to the area where we had last seen the moose. All three of us looked and looked for the animal, but he'd given us the slip by moving into some thick brush. We got back into the airplane and on our way back to the lodge we spotted two really big bull moose fighting each other. Al landed on another lake, and we carefully walked up to where the bulls were fighting. They were so intent on what they were doing they didn't notice us.

Al and I looked over both of the big moose and agreed that the one on the right had the biggest rack. Judy took her time and brought him down with one shot. We did a quick job of cleaning out the moose and flew back to the lodge. Al took his crew back to the site to finish processing and packing out the meat and the rack.

The moose rack measured 64 inches, and Judy ended up with the second-largest moose rack of the season. We took the meat into Anchorage and had it cut and wrapped by Alaska Sausage Company. We couldn't serve moose or caribou to our customers and charge them for it, but quite often some of our customers wanted a taste of caribou or moose meat, so Judy just cooked some wild game for them as a side dish.

Judy and her trophy Caribou

Difficult Decisions

Dick and his wife, Liz, were teacher friends of ours who helped us at the lodge quite often. To help repay them for their help I invited Dick to go hunting for some caribou. We flew a short distance from the lodge and spotted a herd. Dick was a good shot, and he was able to get three nice caribou, which at that time was the limit. I helped him process two of the animals, since I knew I could not haul three caribou and a passenger at the same time. It didn't take me very long to fly back to the lodge with the two caribou we had processed, so I decided to leave behind the survival gear I carried in the airplane.

When I flew back to pick up Dick and the other caribou, fog had settled in over the area where we'd been hunting. I flew back and forth over the area, but couldn't find a break in the fog. I couldn't leave Dick out there overnight, because without survival gear he probably wouldn't have made it through the long night. At this time of year daylight came around ten-thirty in the morning and by two-thirty in the afternoon it was too dark to fly. Temperatures were between 30 and 45 degrees below zero. I knew I'd made a terrible mistake by removing the survival gear from my airplane, and my time was running short to find Dick and still have time to return to the lodge before dark.

I had several short one-way conversations with the Lord and promised I would not fly again if he would just help me find my friend Dick. I made another pass over the area where I thought Dick was, but still couldn't find an opening, so I flew back to Lake Louise and lined up on a cabin I had used as a reference on my original flight to the area where we'd been hunting. I had to fly at treetop level to stay under the fog, and kept telling myself what a dumb cluck I was for leaving my survival gear back at the lodge. Even if I could find Dick I might not have enough time now to land, pick him up, and still take off before the fog really settled in over this small lake.

I lucked out, probably with some divine help, and found Dick anxiously waiting for my return. Upon landing I hollered to him to leave the caribou and get into the plane as fast as he could. The return flight was a white-knuckle trip. The fog was getting lower and I was forced to fly at treetop level. We made it back to Lake Louise and the weather over the lake was clear. From that day on I made sure the survival gear stayed in the airplane.

David Goocey was a young pilot looking for some bush flying experience, and he flew my Super Cub while Al flew the Cessna 180. After Al left the lodge we hired David Goocey as a pilot and handyman. Dave's older brother was one of my former instructors and he'd also given Judy a few introductory flying lessons. Easy-going and quick to get along with customers, David fit into the lodge business quite well. He took excellent care of the Super Cub and he was a careful pilot. For as long as he flew for us he did not put a ding or scratch on the Super Cub.

Rescue

During the winter months we always took our warm clothes with us for the trip to Anchorage. On this particular trip something told me to take extra sleeping bags, just in case something unforeseen happened. The temperature was around 45 degrees below zero when we left the lodge, and the trip was uneventful until we approached a good-sized lake. Something caught my eye and I asked Judy to look out over the lake as I pulled off the side of the road. At first we thought it was some wolves crossing the lake, but as we got closer we could see three people waving frantically.

I stopped the truck to see if we could help, and as they approached the truck we could see they were soaking wet and really cold. They told us they'd been driving on the lake to go ice fishing and the ice broke. They'd gone into the water with the car. Somehow they'd managed to get out of the car, and after several attempts they had crawled up on the ice.

They'd just started walking back to the road when we approached. We put the two adults in the back of the truck and wrapped them up in the extra sleeping bags. The truck had a shell canopy on it, so at least they were out of the wind. The youngster we put up in front with us, and we turned up the heat. I drove as fast as I could to the Palmer hospital, which was quite a few miles away. We checked these folks into the emergency room and they survived the ordeal without any serious frostbite.

I don't know why I put the extra sleeping bags in the truck that day, but I was glad I did, and so were the people we took to the hospital.

Ptarmigan

During the moose and caribou season Gene Needles used our lodge as a base camp for his guiding business. Gene catered to hunters from all over the United States and he had quite a few hunters from Germany.

The hunters Gene had from Germany were usually from the medical profession, doctors and surgeons. We sold hunting and fishing licenses at the lodge, and Judy usually helped the hunters fill out their forms. One of the doctors Gene brought to the lodge spoke only German to Gene and the assistant guides. When Judy sat down with him to fill out his license application she told him she didn't speak German. He said in a very quiet voice that was okay, because he could read and speak English.

Surprised, Judy asked him why he didn't speak English to Gene and the others, and he said he'd learned a long time ago that if he spoke English at a hunting or ski lodge he'd always be badgered by other customers consulting him about sore shoulders, painful backs, or some other medical malady. That was why he refused to speak English on vacation. He went on these vacations to get away from his job for a while, and it refreshed his mind and body to be around healthy people.

Gene also catered to some pretty wealthy businessmen from the United States. Mr. Taylor was one of the businessmen who hunted with Gene every year, and he owned a very large sporting goods distributorship. Every year he came to the lodge he brought the latest in hunting gear, a new hunting rifle or some new gadget. He was a very likable person but he took a lot of kidding, because according to him everything he sold was the best money could buy.

Around the lodge, and especially in the more remote hunting camps, we had a lot of ptarmigan, a bird similar to a grouse, but unique in that it changes color in winter from brown to white. If these birds have not been disturbed they are quite docile. Mr. Taylor had heard that ptarmigan were very good to eat and he wanted to try shooting a few for dinner. Harry was one of the assistant guides working for Gene, and he had an ornery streak.

When Mr. Taylor told Harry that he would like to shoot some ptarmigan for dinner Harry said he'd give him a hand. They walked a little way from the main camp and Harry told Mr. Taylor that in order to make a clean kill on a ptarmigan and not waste any of the meat the hunter had to be and excellent shot. He had to place the shot exactly ¼ inch in front of the ptarmigan's beak. When Mr. Taylor asked why, Harry explained that when the bullet goes by the ptarmigan's beak at such high velocity, it draws the breath right out of the bird and it falls over just long enough for the hunter to catch it without doing any damage to the meat.

I don't know how long Mr. Taylor tried this technique of harvesting ptarmigans, but he sure took a lot of kidding about it.

Our First October

Conducting the business at Evergreen Lodge did not allow us much free time. The lodge business consisted of the following: a marina, air taxi, water taxi, liquor store, grocery store, weather station, boat and snowmachine rental service, a maintenance contract for the Lake Louise airfield, a maintenance contract for the sanitary fill, and a gas station supplying various types of aviation fuel, and gas for boats and cars. In addition to taking care of these aspects of the business we also generated our own power and maintained our water supply and septic system.

We worked together, but at times we hardly had time to talk to each other. We were glad when the month of October came. The lakes started to freeze over and we had to pull the docks out of the water to keep the ice from smashing them during spring breakup. It was also the time to take the boats out of the water, and we had to store the outboard motors.

The first October we were so broke we decided to stay at the lodge. I put up a barricade to block traffic from coming to the lodge, and put up a big sign by the barricade, which said we were closed and would open on November 1.

For the first time in months we were able to sleep in and to have dinner with just the family. A couple of days later people started coming to the lodge. When we told them we were closed they said that was okay because now we would have time to talk to them. They asked what we were going to serve for dinner and we told them, since we were closed to the public we were going to have moose stew. They said that was okay because that's what they wanted to eat anyway. The next question was what cabin do you want us to use? We told them there were no sheets on the beds. That was okay, they said, because they'd brought their own sleeping bags. This went on all during the month of October.

I told Judy that next October we would get a caretaker to watch the lodge and we would go somewhere just to give us some time to catch up with our spirit and not have to talk to anyone or cater to anyone. Quite often our customers told us what a wonderful life we had. Owning a lodge out in a remote area and having an airplane to go hunting and boats to go fishing must be wonderful. The conversation usually ended with remarks like, "When I retire I'm going to buy a lodge." Several times I had to bite my tongue before I told these folks that I purchased the lodge to semi-retire and that I got not only tired but damn tired. To get an idea of what it takes to conduct the business of running a lodge like this, just imagine having an open house at your home seven days a week, twenty-four hours a day, eleven months of the year.

When we bought the lodge we had a ¾ ton pickup truck we used to go to Anchorage to pick up groceries and parts for the generators or for the airplanes and boats. This trip consisted of getting up very early in the morning and driving 180 miles to Anchorage, purchasing the groceries, soda pop, beer, and whatever parts we needed for the lodge. We'd have a quick lunch somewhere and drive the 180 miles back to the lodge. The only things we had delivered to the lodge were fuel oil for the generators and the various types of fuel for the airplanes, boats, or snowmachines, and the propane fuel.

As the business grew, we had to purchase a 1½ ton flatbed truck to haul all the supplies back to the lodge. We bought most of our groceries from a bulk-sale type of grocery store. People would see us checking out several huge carts of food and ask us if we had a big family, or they'd want to know where the party was going to be held. Naturally, we told them about Evergreen Lodge and gave them a brochure.

The first time we hauled groceries from Anchorage to the lodge in the winter we unloaded all the food into the kitchen and went to bed. The next morning we couldn't believe what had happened in the kitchen. The floor was black. The large sack of potatoes we had purchased had frozen on the way and when they thawed out they'd turned into a black liquid. That was the last time we tried to haul real potatoes to the lodge in winter. From then on Judy used dehydrated potatoes.

We also found out that the beer and soda pop would freeze and go flat. When we asked the distributors about it they told us to store the frozen cases upside down until we used them. This seemed to do the trick, but now and then we still got a case of beer or soda pop that went flat.

The Kentuckians

One summer day while I was working on the docks a car with a Kentucky license plate drove up to the boat-launching ramp. Two guys and a nice-looking lady came over to talk to me. They asked if I knew of any land around Lake Louise that they could homestead. I told them as far as I knew all the land around the three lakes was either privately owned or it was owned by the government. The lady asked me if the lake froze over in winter, and she also wanted to know if it froze hard enough to drive a car on it. I told her the lake did indeed freeze over in winter, and in a severe winter the ice would be thick enough to drive a D-8 Caterpillar on it.

They looked around a little more and drove off. A few days later they returned and asked if they could park their car at the lodge for a few days. I told them we charged a dollar a day for parking, and they agreed to pay the fee. Several days later they came back and said they'd found a place not too far from the lodge where they were going to build a log cabin. I warned them that they were probably trespassing on someone's property, but that didn't seem to discourage them.

They told us it had been a dream of the boys, who were brothers, to come to Alaska to homestead and build a log cabin they could live in. I showed them the log cabins Bill Poe had built for us. The lady's name was Nancy, and she was married to the one named Walter. The other brother, Jim, was also married, but his wife had stayed in Kentucky.

We didn't see the Kentuckians for quite a while and when they showed up all three were as clean and tidy as anyone living with all the modern conveniences. They told us they'd been hard at work building their cabin and digging out a root cellar, and they wanted to know if we could use some help, since they'd be willing to work for groceries and other supplies.

We couldn't have hired a harder-working crew than these three. Judy put Kentucky Nancy to work in the kitchen and she also helped with the laundry and making beds in the cabins. Walt and Jim helped me install some power poles around the lodge parking lot. These two guys were not afraid to work and I enjoyed working with both of them. They worked for us for several days and in exchange we traded them an airtight wood stove and some groceries and other supplies.

While working with Walt and Jim I learned that their father was superintendent of a school system in Kentucky, and it had been their boyhood dream to come to Alaska. We asked them to show us where their cabin was on the map, so that if we needed additional help we could fly over to their cabin site. They had purposefully located their cabin on a very small lake so that a plane could not land near their cabin. All three used backpacks to transport their stove and groceries back to the cabin, which was approximately eight miles from the lodge.

The Kentuckians came to help us several more times during the summer with various jobs around the lodge. We trusted them enough to have them stay at the lodge when we both had to make a trip to Anchorage.

During the hunting season we needed some extra help, so Dave Goocey and I flew over their cabin site. We buzzed the cabin and when they came out we dropped a note attached to a rock asking them to give us a hand at the lodge. They read the note and acknowledged that they would be available. A few hours later they showed up at the lodge looking as clean and scrubbed as before.

At Christmastime we invited the Kentuckians to the lodge to share Christmas with us. Walt brought me a beautiful fox pelt. Judy had taught Nancy to knit and she'd knitted several gifts for us. Jim stayed at the cabin to make sure things didn't freeze up.

Intuition

During our second summer at the lodge I had all the cabins converted to propane heat instead of the old army surplus oil burners. The propane heaters burned clean and our customers liked them because they didn't leave an oil smell in the cabins. The propane heaters also had a blower system, which helped circulate the heat.

One weekend in November most of the cabins were rented, and during the night the temperature dropped to 50 degrees below zero. I heard a lot of pounding on the outside door and got up to check it out. The customers wanted to come into the lodge because they said the heaters in their cabins would not work. I woke Judy up and she started to make coffee in the 100-cup coffeepot. I found out also that the propane heaters in the lodge weren't working.

Al Gruchow and his family were staying at the lodge, and he got up and started a fire in the fireplace to get some heat in the building. Judy tried to cook some breakfast for the guests, but the propane stove didn't work, either.

We couldn't raise anyone on the high-frequency radio, so I had no choice but to try and start my pickup truck and drive 20 miles out to the highway to a regular telephone. I heated the engine on the GMC pickup for half an hour or so and was able to get it started. In seven years at the lodge, helping twenty or more people each winter weekend to preheat and start their vehicles, I'd found that a General Motors vehicle would start much more easily than any other.

I drove out to the highway and called Terry, our propane distributor, who lived in Glennallen. I told him we had a serious problem. None of the propane heaters were working and quite a few guests were not only cold but hungry as well. Terry agreed to come out to the lodge to see what he could do to get the heaters working. When I got back to the lodge everyone was talking about the chimney fire. While people were standing around trying to get warm, they'd kept putting a few more small logs on the fire. Evidently, the creosote that had built up in the chimney had caught fire.

Thank goodness Al Gruchow and his friend, Bobby, were awake. Both of them grabbed fire extinguishers; Al scrambled up the ladder to the roof and discharged the extinguisher down the chimney wile Bobby discharged the other extinguisher up into the chimney from below. Together they put out the fire.

Terry came to the lodge with his propane truck, and he filled the 1,000-gallon tank. The propane heaters in the cabins and in the lodge now started to work, and the customers were satisfied now that they had heat in their cabins. Some went back to bed.

Terry and I had a long discussion about the properties of propane fuel, and he told me that propane drops back to a liquid state at 45 degrees below zero. This type of heating system was not going to work, because the temperatures could drop to at least 65 degrees below zero during the winter months. It was decision time. We either had to replace all the propane heaters and switch back to oil burner heaters or find a solution to keep the propane heaters working at these extreme temperatures. Terry said he'd discuss it with his supervisors.

A few days later Terry delivered another 1,000-gallon propane tank to the lodge. After his discussion with his supervisors they had decided to install two 1,000-gallon tanks and build an insulated shed over the two tanks. They figured that with insulation the tanks would continue to produce gas, and it would not revert to liquid form.

One of Terry's supervisors delivered the necessary building supplies and he built and insulated the shed. I added one safety factor:

a metal pass-through into the shed. With this pass-through I would be able to use my 50,000-BTU oil burner space heater and a piece of flexible metal pipe to heat the shed if the propane dropped out on me again.

The insulated shed cured the problem until January 1971 when the temperature dropped to almost 80 degrees below zero. I was glad I had planned ahead, because I had to heat the shed to keep the propane working. At the same time, I was concerned about the fuel for my generator, because the flow point on the generator fuel was guaranteed only to 70 degrees below zero.

I was also thankful that I'd had enough sense to build a garage attached to my heated workshop. By cutting a door into the workshop building to allow enough heat to flow into the garage I kept my truck warm in case of another emergency.

Some folks say that I am intuitive, and perhaps that is true. On Thanksgiving day, Jan Listoe, a young man who worked for us, and Jim Freeman, a customer, were riding snowmachines on Lake Louise. Jim hit a bump in the snow and he was thrown off. He was not wearing a helmet, and he must have hit his head pretty hard, because Jan told us that when Jim got back on the snowmachine he kept going around in circles. Jan tried to stop him but in vain.

Jan drove his snowmachine to the lodge and told us what had happened. Thank goodness I had built the garage, because the truck was warm and I was able to start it without preheating. Judy and Jan got into the warm truck and drove out to find Jim. I drove a snowmachine and we found Jim out on the lake still going around in circles. I thought I was going to have to lasso him to get him to stop but for some reason when I hollered at him he stopped.

We put him into the truck and stopped by the lodge to get a mattress to put in the back of the truck. We laid Jim down on the mattress and Judy stayed in the back with him. I drove the 50 miles to the Glennallen hospital as fast as I could. Doctors checked Jim over and said he had a light concussion and he could return to the lodge. They also recommended that all of us wear helmets while riding snowmachines. On the way back to the lodge Jim told us he knew he would be okay when he looked up from the mattress and saw Judy's blue eyes looking at him. We took the doctors' advice and all of us purchased helmets for use on the snowmachines.

One of our log cabins at 45° below zero

Bozo

M ike and Alma agreed to stay at the lodge again for the month of October while we took a break and went to Matzalan, Mexico. We enjoyed the warm weather in Mexico and chartered a boat to take us deep-sea fishing. The captain of the boat put us on some fine fishing; we caught several dorado and I landed a nice sailfish. We gave most of the fish to the boat crew and took some back to the motel. The restaurant at the motel cooked the dorado for us and it was excellent.

We met a taxicab driver by the name of Bernardo who spoke Spanish and English. Bernardo gave us a comprehensive tour of the various developments around Matzalan. Every time we needed a cab we asked for Bernardo. He took us to several open-air markets and at one of the markets I found a leather belt I wanted. I told the salesperson I liked the belt and would come back later to buy it.

The salesperson kept dropping the price of the belt until I could not resist. I paid the lady for the belt and she smiled at me and said something in Spanish that sounded very pleasant. I looked at Bernardo, who had a smirk on his face. When we walked away from the salesperson I asked Bernardo what the lady had said. He told me that in a loose translation she'd told me, "May a seagull take a liking to your sombrero."

We had a very good vacation and it was nice not to think about the lodge business. After ten days we were rested and decided to fly to Orlando, Florida, to visit Judy's folks. We went to the travel agent to change our tickets. It was a very hot day, and we purchased some soda pop. When the agent asked us if we wanted ice in our sodas we accepted without thinking.

Until then we had been very careful not to drink any water except the bottled variety, and we'd avoided brushing our teeth with water from the faucet. It didn't take long for all of us to get a good dose of Montezuma's revenge. We took the medication we had with us, but we still used a lot of bathrooms between Matzalan, Orlando, Chicago, and Anchorage. After that experience we did not go back to Mexico for several years.

When we got back to the lodge at the end of October the really cold weather had not arrived yet, and the ice on the lakes was still very thin. Mike and Alma filled us in on what had happened around the lake, and related this story to us.

It had been quiet around the lodge, since the lakes were just starting to freeze over. One day while they were sitting in the lodge Alma thought she heard a dog barking and whimpering. Mike went outside to investigate and spotted Bozo, our black Labrador, across the bay. Bozo had fallen through the thin ice and she was struggling in the water and trying to get up on the ice. From Mike's description Bozo was making such a pitiful sound that chills ran up and down his spine.

He told Alma he was going to do his best to rescue Bozo. He put on some warm clothes and went down to the lake where we kept the canoe, and dragged the canoe around the lake until he was fairly close to the dog.

Mike put one leg in the canoe and used his other leg to push himself across the thin ice until he could reach Bozo. When he got there, the dog had just about given up, and all she could do was whimper. Mike was successful in getting Bozo into the canoe and pushed himself and Bozo back across the ice until they reached the shoreline. He took the dog up to the lodge and got her warmed up.

We thanked Mike and Alma over and over again for saving Bozo, because she was one of the best-behaved dogs we had ever owned. It took several weeks before Bozo would go out on the ice again.

Caribou Rescue

A few days after Mike and Alma returned to Anchorage, we watched a couple of caribou walking across the lake. The ice was still thin so we were curious. We'd always heard that caribou would not fall through the ice because somehow they always sensed the danger of thin ice.

We watched the two animals as they got closer and we could not believe our eyes as they both fell through the ice. We watched a little longer and figured the caribou would somehow be able to get back up on the ice, but it seemed that the more the larger of the two struggled, the more it kept breaking off the ice, and it could not get out of the water. I remembered what Mike had told us about his rescue efforts on behalf of Bozo, so I put on my float coat and got a long piece of rope. I dragged the canoe out onto the ice, put one leg inside and propelled myself across the ice by pushing with the other. As I got closer to the caribou, the larger one seemed to be weakening and wasn't making much of an effort to get up on the ice.

I tried to lasso the smaller caribou several times before I got the loop around its neck. I didn't want to pull too hard because I was afraid to strangle the little one. Finally I was able to put enough pressure on the rope to pull the smaller animal out of the water and up on the ice.

Just as I relaxed the pull on the rope the little bugger jumped back into the water, where his mother was giving up the struggle. I got him up on the ice for the second time and kept pulling him toward the canoe. When I got him close enough I was able to tie his legs and put him into the canoe.

I dragged the canoe and the caribou to the beach and over to my heated shop.. Judy and our daughter had watched the rescue from the lodge, and they brought some old towels to the shop. I kept the caribou tied up until we rubbed him down and dried him off.

After all that effort I didn't want anyone to shoot him, so I tied a couple of strands of orange surveyor's tape around his neck. We took him out of the warm shop and turned him loose. He didn't stay around very long and headed off into the woods.

Long Island

Late one summer an older couple came into the lodge and asked about a guided hunting trip for moose and Dall sheep. We explained that we were air taxi operators, but we did not offer a guide service.

As we talked about sheep hunting and moose hunting they told us they were from Long Island, which was evident from their accent. Mr. Willums really wanted to go hunting for Dall sheep and moose. We told them several guides used our lodge as a base camp for their hunters, but most of them booked their hunts a year or two in advance.

Mr. Hugh Willums was pretty heavy-set, and he practically chain-smoked cigars. But he had a peculiar habit–he smoked the cigars to only half their length. We kidded him about being popular with the bums. His wife told us that when they traveled they always packed one suitcase full of cigars.

Hugh and his wife stayed for several days, and we found out that Mrs. Willums had been a chef in one of New York's major hotels. She wanted something to do, so she offered to help Judy in the kitchen. I told Hugh I'd try to line him up with a guide, and I invited him to drive out to the highway with me to check our mail and see if Al Lee, a local guide, could take him hunting.

I introduced Hugh to Al Lee. Al couldn't take him sheep hunting, but he would take him moose hunting if he got into a little better shape. Hugh wanted to know what he had to do, so Al told him that when he could walk from Evergreen Lodge to the Lake Louise airport and back, he'd take him hunting. The total distance was about 4 miles.

Hugh started his training program the next day. He cut back on the number of cigars he smoked and he started his walking routine. The first day he didn't get too far, but he didn't give up.

Mrs. Willums enjoyed working in the kitchen with Judy and she was amazed at how determined Hugh was to go hunting. It took him a week or so before he could walk to the airport and back to the lodge. Al stopped by several times to check on Hugh and he was pleased to hear of his progress.

We helped to outfit Hugh and he was off for a few days of hunting with Al. It was beginning to get colder, and the northern lights were out. We told Mrs. Willums about the northern lights and how they danced across the skies in a splendid show of beautiful colors. She told us that no matter when they showed up, she wanted to see them. The very next evening the temperature dropped a little more and the northern lights put on a fantastic display. Judy went to the cabin where Mrs. Willums was staying and woke her up. Mrs. Willums was awed at how beautiful they were and how quickly they could disappear. Hugh got his moose and a caribou, and he was so pleased with his experience that he promised that both of them would return the following year.

Honeymoon Couple

It was a beautiful summer day when a very young couple who had just been married came to the lake to spend a few days on their honeymoon. Some friends of theirs were letting them use their cabin on Lake Louise.

They packed a lot of groceries and a few beers with them in their boat and they headed down the lake to their friends' cabin. We didn't hear anything about them for a few days. Then one day we got a very distressed call on the citizens band radio.

It was Millie Hayes, one of our customers, who called and in a very excited voice asked us to come to the newlywed couple's cabin because the young man was in the outhouse and he was bleeding very badly. Judy and I conferred for a bit and thought that possibly he had a serious problem with hemorrhoids, or maybe he had some internal bleeding.

We gathered up a bunch of towels and some other items. Fred Laufenberger was flying out of the lodge at this time, and we decided that Fred and Judy would fly down and I would take my jet boat, which was very fast, and we'd meet at the cabin. By the time Fred warmed up the airplane I was already at the cabin site.

I beached the boat and ran up to the outhouse, but I couldn't find anyone, nor did I see any blood. By this time Fred and Judy were right behind me and we headed for the cabin. The moment I got inside I spotted the young man on the floor. I ran over to him, and I was stunned. A massive amount of blood was on the floor, and there was a bullet wound in his head. We checked him for any signs of life, but as far as we could determine he was dead. The young man had a gun belt and an empty holster wrapped around his shoulder, and on the floor next to him was a pistol.

We went over to Millie's cabin and told her what we'd found. Millie was also a nurse, and she did her best to comfort the young woman. She had come running barefoot to Millie's cabin, and in a hysterical voice told Millie that her husband was bleeding very badly. Millie thought the girl told her he was in the outhouse.

Fred and Judy flew back to the lodge and Judy was able to make contact with the Alaska State Troopers. They dispatched an officer to investigate the accident.

We talked to Millie about the incident a few days later, and she said the young woman had told her that when a friend of theirs heard that they were going to a cabin on a remote lake, he insisted that her husband borrow his pistol for protection. He wanted them to take a weapon because he had just read a story about a young couple vacationing at a cabin on a remote lake, and someone had broken in and raped the girl.

The newlywed husband didn't want to take the gun because he didn't know anything about guns, but to please his friend he'd taken the gun with him.

The young wife told Millie that it was such a warm and beautiful day that her husband had decided to have a beer and take a nap. He put the gun belt with the holster and pistol over his shoulder, and since the refrigerator was low to the floor, he had to bend over to get a beer out. Evidently, when he bent over the pistol dropped out of the holster, and when the hammer hit the floor it caused the pistol to discharge a bullet, which caused the fatal accident.

Marshall

O ne summer day a floatplane landed and taxied up to the dock.
Two guys got out and walked up to the lodge. I recognized
the pilot as the husband of one of my former teachers. He introduced his friend as Marshall Johnson.

We exchanged pleasantries, and Marshall asked me where he
could get some drinking water. I thought that was a strange question, so I told him the lake was full of it. He looked at me kind of
funny, so I explained to him that we drew our water from the lake,
but since we were a commercial operation, we had to add chlorine
to the water to satisfy the health department.

A few months later Marshall purchased a piece of property and
a cabin on Lake Susitna. He kept his boat on our dock, so we got
to see him and his wife, Bonnie, almost every weekend. As time
went by we learned that Marshall worked for a radio station in
Anchorage, and his wife worked in the court system. He asked me
what type of advertising we did for the lodge, and I told him we
had a very simple brochure. We learned that he sold advertising
for the radio station, and that he was the person in the airplane
who gave the rush hour traffic report.

We worked out some trades, and Marshall started to do some
advertising for Evergreen Lodge in conjunction with his traffic
report. We didn't notice any increase in our business, so Marshall
came up with the idea of negative advertising. Every time Marshall
would try to say *Evergreen Lodge on Lake Louise*, someone at the
studio would push a buzzer to blank out the name.

Marshall got quite creative about getting the name of the lodge
on the air. He'd start out with, "The traffic on Northern Lights

Boulevard has stopped, but now that the light has turned Evergreen Lodge . . ." Of course, it was prearranged that a person at the station would push the buzzer to try and keep him from saying the name of the lodge.

The next day on the traffic report Marshall said, "The weather looks clear and I can see all the way to Evergreen Lodge on Lake Louise." The buzzer sounded again in an attempt to block the mention of the lodge.

This turned out to be a successful advertising program, and people from all around the area started to send Marshall ideas on how to say *Evergreen Lodge* before the buzzer sounded.

Quite a few people drove up from Anchorage and the surrounding area to find out what was so terrible about Evergreen Lodge and why the name could not be mentioned on the traffic report. The advertising campaign was a success–it brought people to the lodge.

Marshall was not a true believer in the spirit of giving Christmas gifts, but I decided during the holidays to give him and his wife a present anyway. I found a commercial-type toilet seat, the kind that looks like a horseshoe. I scrubbed it up and asked Judy to knit a couple of pairs of tube socks that we could slip over both sides of the toilet seat. Judy had some bright-colored yarn and knit two sleeves that fit over the seat.

We wrapped up the gift and gave it to Marshall and Bonnie. They said they appreciated the gift, because at 30 or 40 degrees below zero you think long and hard about the trip to the outhouse. They kept the seat in their cabin to keep it warm until they made the final decision to go to the outhouse. This made the trip a little more comfortable. At least they could sit on a warm seat.

Whitey

Prior to our purchase of the lodge, my instructor, Ed Broome, and I flew up to Gunsight Mountain Lodge. We had planned to look over some of the surrounding area but the fog grounded us. We had dinner at the Gunsight, and we had a chance to talk to Whitey, the lodge owner. Whitey was an experienced pilot, so we took the opportunity to ask him a lot of questions about bush flying.

Both of us had heard about overflow and how dangerous it can be to a person who has to walk through it. Whitey explained that overflow occurs when the lakes first start to freeze over. When lakes freeze but the ice does not get very thick before it snows, the weight of the snow causes the ice to sink, and water is forced up through fissures in the ice. The snow acts as insulation, and does not allow the water that is on top of the ice to freeze.

This can be hazardous to anyone walking on a lake with overflow. People walking onto the lake step through the snow and into the water trapped below the snow on top of the ice. As they walk on and bring their wet boots up out of the trapped water, the cold air changes the water to ice on their boots. More ice freezes to the boots with every step, and pretty soon a size 10 boot turns into a 14, and, of course, it begins to weigh more.

In time, walking through the overflow can become life threatening. As ice continues to form on a person's boots, the boots become too large and too heavy to walk in. It becomes physically impossible to go any further and the person will more than likely freeze to death.

Whitey further explained what a pilot must do prior to landing on a lake with overflow. If he suspects that a lake has overflow on it, he will touch down lightly on the skis and then immediately add full power to take off again. Then he makes a low pass over his ski tracks to see if any green color shows up in the snow. If it does, that's a good indication that overflow is present.

In order to land under such conditions, Whitey outlined several procedures. By now Ed and I were eager to hear about them. He'd had good luck landing on lakes with overflow, he told us. His procedure was to keep as much power on as needed to keep the plane moving at a pretty good pace after landing until he had a chance to taxi up on dry land. It was important once the plane stopped to get out as fast as possible and break a few limbs from a tree. After putting the small limbs in front of his skis he taxis up on the limbs to keep the wet skis from freezing to the ground. Skis freezing to the ground or in the overflow are almost impossible to break free.

Another technique Whitey told us about was the use of visqueen. He recommended that we always include visqueen in our survival gear. It could be used to make a temporary shelter and he had also used it to take off from a lake with overflow on it.

That method was sort of supplementary to the first one. He explained that once the skis are up on the small limbs he takes the visqueen and cuts strips a little wider and longer than the skis on his airplane. Next he ties a knot in one end of the plastic, slips it over the front tip of the ski, and tucks the visqueen under the skis to give them a slippery surface. This allows him to take off a little more easily over the overflow. Once the plane is airborne, the visqueen usually tears off by itself.

We really enjoyed talking to Whitey, and since there was no one else around I think he enjoyed talking to us. I asked him if he'd had any unusual experiences that he could tell us about. This is the story he told us.

Whitey was a guide who catered to trophy hunters, and to satisfy these hunters he had to do some pretty risky bush flying. He'd strip everything he could off his airplane to make it lighter, such as the battery, the starter, and any instrument he felt he didn't need.

Like a lot of other guides, Whitey would search for a location close to a good hunting area where he cleared the area of rocks or trees or brush to create a small runway. Sometimes he spent hours or weeks clearing the area so he could land his plane. Afterward he'd fly in a few extra cans of aviation fuel. Just before hunting season one year he landed on one of these remote strips to check his supply of aviation fuel. He said he couldn't believe that only one can had any fuel in it.

He flew back to his lodge and filled up the empty gas cans. Then he flew the gas cans back to his remote strip and put a sign by them: "One gas can is contaminated." He figured this would discourage anyone from using his gas supply.

The next time he flew back to that strip another surprise awaited him. Someone had changed his sign. It now read, "Two gas cans are contaminated."

Cessna 180 on wheels

Air Taxi

In order to keep our air taxi permit valid we were required to keep a commercial pilot around at all times, and our aircraft had to be inspected every hundred hours by a licensed aircraft and engine mechanic. Private pilots are required only to have their aircraft inspected yearly. At the lodge we were also subject to unannounced inspections each year. The FAA inspectors went over our manuals and made sure we had updated them all. This made sense to me, because in effect we were running a small airline. In jest we called our air taxi Polish Sausage Airline, because most of the caribou the hunters harvested was made into Polish sausage.

Our moose and caribou season opened in August and we were busy with our regular dock customers, boat rentals, and our efforts to accommodate the guides who were using our lodge as a base camp for their hunters.

On a couple of boat trips I had to make around the lake I noticed an airplane that was operating out of a campground near Army Point. I didn't recognize the plane, so I asked Judy if she knew anything about it. She told me that two hunters had come into the lodge and said they were going to fly out for a moose hunt with some guy operating out of the camp he had set up near Army Point. Judy asked them if he was a friend of theirs and they said no, but the guy had told them he was an air taxi operator and his rates were lower than those at Evergreen Lodge.

I asked one of our customers to go over and check things out for me. Upon his return he told me the pilot was not a guide, nor was he a commercial pilot. The man had told him he just wanted to make a few bucks flying hunters out for moose and caribou.

I called the office in Anchorage that issued our air taxi permit, and complained about what sounded like an illegal air taxi operation our area. They assured me that someone would look into the problem. A week went by and the guy was still conducting his business.

Judy and I made a special trip to Anchorage and stopped by the FAA office to file a written complaint about the illegal operator. Again they assured us they would send someone to check things out. A few days later a portly man and his young son came into the lodge and the man told us he was here to check out the alleged illegal operation at Army Point. He specifically pointed out to me that he was traveling incognito, and asked where Army Point was, and what was the best way to get there.

I showed him the location and he decided that to further disguise his identity he wanted to rent a boat and pretend that he and his son were fishing. We rented him a boat, and when he returned a couple of hours later I asked him if he had documented the flights that were being made by the Cessna 180. He looked at me with a puzzled look on his face and told me he didn't know the difference between a Super Cub and a Cessna 180. He looked even more embarrassed when he told me his son had fallen out of the boat.

I suggested to him that perhaps he should drive over to Army Point and jot down the number on the airplane and the number of times the pilot took off with customers. He agreed to do that, but we didn't see or hear from him again.

This really frustrated me, because we were doing our best to operate the air taxi business according to their regulations, but this office would not do anything about a "bandit" operation. The pilot did not have a commercial license, nor did he have his aircraft inspected every hundred hours of operating time, and most likely he didn't carry any liability insurance.

When the FAA inspector showed up to inspect our manuals again, I told them about the bandit operation that had gone on for several weeks at Army Point. They just didn't have enough personnel to check up on all the air taxi violations they said, but when I told them I had seriously considered tearing up my air taxi permit and operating like the other bandits, they warned me that it would not be wise for me to do that. When they caught me I'd have to pay a big fine.

Helicopter

It was a very blustery day and the lake was rough. As I looked out the window I thought I saw a big splash, and what looked like a boat heading toward the lodge. I pointed this out to several customers and when I looked through the binoculars I could see a boat that was taking a pounding in the waves.

The boat made its way to the dock and we recognized it as one that belonged to John Stephensen, who was one of our boat dock customers. John tied up his boat and came running up the hill to the lodge. He told us his wife was asthmatic and she was having a difficult time breathing. He wanted our pilot to fly down to his cabin with Judy to see what Judy could do for his wife.

The lake was too rough to attempt a takeoff in the float plane, so we used the high-frequency radio to contact our answering service in Anchorage, told them about the medical emergency, and had them get in touch with the Glennallen hospital. After a while we were told the helicopter was on its way to the lodge, and the pilot was bringing some medication for Mrs. Stephensen.

It didn't take long before we heard the helicopter approaching. I directed the chopper to a place to land, and as he landed he shouted at me. He wanted to know if I was the nurse that he was supposed to pick up. By that time Judy was standing next to me and when I asked her where John was she told me he was afraid to go back to his cabin because he thought his wife might have died.

Judy directed the pilot to John's cabin, gave Mrs. Stephensen the medication the hospital had sent, and with the pilot's assistance helped the patient into the helicopter. The pilot took off in the wrong direction, so Judy tapped him on the shoulder and shouted at him to turn around and head toward the Glenn Highway and the hospital. She said she was quite relieved when they got to the hospital and the pilot landed the helicopter. The hospital staff took Mrs. Stephensen inside and under their care she fully recovered.

The pilot offered to fly Judy back to the lodge, but she politely refused the offer. On the flight to the hospital she had noticed that a lot of the instruments on the chopper were taped over, so she asked the pilot about it. He told her that some of the instruments did not work, so he'd taped them over to keep people from asking questions. A week or so later we heard that this pilot had crashed because he'd run out of fuel. He had broken both legs but survived the crash.

John Stephensen drove his car up to the Glennallen hospital to pick up his wife. A week or so later John and his wife returned to the lodge and thanked us for coordinating the helicopter flight.

Beard

While Tom was building the insulated shed for the propane tanks, we got around to talking about growing a beard. I grew a full beard in the winter months to help keep my face from getting frostbitten. I enjoyed growing a beard, because as a principal quite often I'd had to shave twice a day if I had to attend a meeting or be in attendance at a school function in the evening.

I told Tom of an experience I'd had with a full beard. I had shot a moose and the temperature was around 30 degrees below zero. I was in a hurry to clean out the entrails, trying to hurry up the job of cutting up the moose so that I could haul it back to the lodge in my airplane.

The harder I worked and exhaled, the more ice formed on my mustache and beard. Pretty soon it felt like someone was pulling on my beard with both hands, and my eyes started to tear up. Not only was my face hurting, but I was concerned that pretty soon I wouldn't be able to see well enough to fly back to the lodge, since the tears turned to ice on my glasses.

I packed as much moose meat as I could carry back to the airplane, and I was fortunate that it started right up. I flew back to the lodge and headed for the nearest heater. After I thawed out my beard and melted the ice off my glasses, I took a pair of scissors and cut off the beard. The following day I flew over to the lake where I'd shot the moose and finished cutting it up and hauling it back to the lodge.

After I told Tom this story he just laughed. I told him it was not funny and I'd been in serious trouble. He assured me he was laughing in sympathy, and then told me his story. He'd been hunting for caribou with some friends, and he also wore a full beard. He shot a caribou, and after he cleaned out the entrails he started to drag the animal back to their camp.

The temperature was about 25 or 30 degrees below zero and like me, the more he exhaled the more ice formed on his beard. When he got to camp he was in pain, but he was afraid to lean over a fire to melt the ice because he thought his beard might catch on fire. He figured that if he crawled into his sleeping bag he might generate enough heat to thaw his beard. In the sleeping bag he got nice and warm, and he fell asleep. When he woke up he tried to get out of the bag, but he couldn't do it. The ice in his beard had melted and then refrozen to the sleeping bag. His friends heard his groans and when they found out what had happened they cut the sleeping bag away from his face.

The following winter I decided to grow another beard. During the winter months the beard was comfortable and not very itchy. As the weather warmed up, the beard started to itch and I trimmed it and then shaved it off. I had worn my beard in winter, but one night I decided to shave it off. Judy had already gone to bed and didn't know my plan. Early in the morning she rolled over in bed and noticed that my face looked very pale. She thought I had died in my sleep, so she started slapping my face with her hand, to see if she could revive me. I woke up in total confusion. I didn't know if we were being robbed, or if the lodge was on fire. From that time forward I made it a point to tell Judy when I was going to shave off my beard.

Winter Flying

Flying an airplane in the winter months in Alaska can be quite a challenge. First of all the engine has to be preheated so that it will be warm enough to start. A lot of pilots use a small catalytic heater that can be placed inside the engine compartment. It is also quite common to use an insulated engine cover to help with the heating process.

The first time I used a small catalytic heater I went out to check my Super Cub every hour to make sure it did not catch on fire or blow up. Another essential part of winter flying is the use of a pair of wing covers. The wing covers keep snow and frost off the wings. If ice forms on the wings, there is a good possibility that the wings will stall in flight, and a serious accident could occur.

The Super Cub I owned was painted white with a little bit of red trim. I learned the hard way that this was not the best color combination for winter flying. This became painfully clear one winter when I needed to make a phone call to Anchorage to coordinate some things for a snowmachine race we were sponsoring. The high-frequency radio was not working properly, so I decided to fly over to Tolsona Lake to make the call. I preheated the engine and scraped the wings the best I could to remove the snow and frost. I started my takeoff and as I got just a few feet off the runway, the left wing stalled. Luckily I was able to land without any damage to the airplane. Being stubborn, I used a piece of coarse rope to burnish the wings and the leading edge of the wings. I tried another takeoff and the right wing stalled or quit flying as I got a few feet off the runway. Again I was able to land without doing any damage to the plane. Evidently, the conditions were just right to allow frost to form on the wings as fast as I could scrape it off, and it wasn't always easily visible.

If I'd had a bucket of black paint, at this point I would have painted the entire airplane black. A few days later the weather pattern changed and a friend of mine flew the plane to Anchorage. I had the wings painted a dark red with he leading edges black. I could tell if frost or ice had formed on the wings now. I also purchased a set of good wing covers.

Yes, winter flying can be a challenge. But it can also be very enjoyable. The air seems to be smoother and when the lakes are frozen, every lake becomes a potential landing strip. A lot of pilots used our lodge as a base camp for their hunters, and in the winter months I plowed most of the snow off the ice to create a runway in front of the lodge. To give the pilots some depth perception upon landing I lined the sides of the runway with the limbs of evergreen trees.

One year we had an exceptionally mild winter as the temperatures stayed around 20 or 30 degrees below zero instead of the typical 45 to 65 degrees below. The presence of a lot of caribou in the surrounding area attracted many hunters.

Mr. Draze was a pilot who came to the lodge quite often; he was reliable as a person and experienced as a pilot. He told me that he was going to hunt for caribou in an area called the Caribou Hills. I made a mental note of this, and when he did not show up for dinner, I knew I'd have to look for him early the next morning.

Early the next day I flew over to the Caribou Hills and started looking for Mr. Draze. I spotted his airplane on a small lake and as I circled around the lake, he signaled for me to land. After I taxied up to him, he told me he'd removed the tail wheel from his airplane and replaced it with the tail ski because he thought he would be able to get off a little quicker that way. The tail ski did not create as much drag as a wheel.

He had landed on the lake without any problem, but when he started his takeoff he had to taxi around a couple of times to get up enough airspeed to get off the ground. When he taxied around the lake a second time, the snow got stirred up enough so that he could not see where he was going. He pulled back on the stick and expected the plane to stop within a relatively short distance, as it always did with the tail wheel setup. However, the tail ski setup did not dig into the snow, and the plane did not stop until one of the skis ran into a snowbank.

The plane wasn't seriously damaged, and since Mr. Draze carried survival gear he made it through the night without any significant problems. He did a quick but temporary repair job, which consisted of using some wire and the ever handy duct tape, a product we call Super Cub tape.

I took off before him, and told him I would fly cover for him and call him on the radio if I saw anything unusual happening to his airplane. Mr. Draze made a successful takeoff and I followed him to Lake Louise. He seemed to be heading the wrong way, so I called him and told him the lodge was off to his left. The next thing I knew he landed his plane almost immediately. When I called to ask the reason for the sudden landing, he said all he'd understood from my call was that his left wing was coming off.

We made it back to the lodge without any further problems. If you aren't familiar with flying an airplane equipped with skis–there are no brakes on the skis. Upon landing the pilot has to judge about how far the plane will travel before it stops.

The runway I maintained in front of the lodge was approximately 2,000 feet long. One day as we were sitting down for lunch we watched a plane make an approach to the runway, and it seemed to be coming in a little fast. The runway was pretty well packed, and when the pilot touched down he was still going pretty fast. He was, in fact, going so fast that he used up the entire runway and ended up going up the hill about halfway to the lodge. We were able to help him turn the airplane around and he got it back to the runway. We kidded him a lot about the fact that we weren't a drive-in lodge.

Al Burnett also provided us with some excitement one day. He called on the radio, which was unusual, because depending on weather conditions the radio would work one day but not the next. He said he'd torn off a ski on takeoff and he wanted the runway cleared so that he could make an attempt to land the Cessna 185 on just one ski.

We moved all the aircraft and snowmachines out of his way, and shortly after that Al made a low pass over the runway. He made a long, slow approach and touched down on one ski. The airplane stayed straight on course until the ski support leg dug into the runway. Then it spun around like a top. No one was hurt but it took a while to get the airplane repaired. Al said that while he was taking off he must have hit a frozen muskrat push-up.

When the lakes freeze over, muskrats keep a hole open in the ice by taking the vegetation that grows on the bottom of the lake and pushing it up through the hole in the ice. When it snows a foot or more, these push-ups are covered, and if you hit one of them with a ski they can do serious damage to an airplane.

Jinx

I had a bad case of the flu and I didn't want to sit around and talk to anyone, so I suggested to Judy that we take a ride out to the highway to check our mail. On the way out a car passed us going toward the lodge, but we didn't recognize it.

We picked up the mail and started back when we saw a car parked along the side of the road. It was starting to get dark, and it was around 40 degrees below zero. I stopped the pickup truck to see if anyone was in the vehicle, but I noticed there were two sets of footprints leading away from the vehicle. One set of tracks was fairly large, and the other was much smaller.

From where the car was parked, it would be about a 12- to 15-mile walk to the lodge. I told Judy what I'd seen, and I speeded up to see if we could overtake the people who were walking. A couple of miles down the road we saw a man and a woman walking. They were dressed in regular street clothes, and they were definitely not prepared for the cold weather.

When I stopped the truck to talk to them, the man said their car had broken down and they were trying to get to Evergreen Lodge. I told them who we were and offered to take them to the lodge. I gave the man my big construction parka and he got into the back of the truck. We put the lady in front next to the heater, and I started back to the lodge.

A few miles down the road a huge gray wolf jumped out onto the road. I stopped the truck as fast as I could, pulled my rifle out and shot the wolf. I didn't say anything to the man in the back of the truck when I put the wolf in the truck bed.

We took the couple inside the lodge, close to a heater to warm them up, and Judy got them a cup of hot coffee and something to eat. After they warmed up a little they introduced themselves as Mr. and Mrs. Fox. They had recently moved to Anchorage and had heard a lot about Evergreen Lodge, so they'd decided to drive up.

After Mr. Fox stopped shivering he told me he didn't know whether the shivering came from the cold or from his recent experience. He said he was thankful for the ride, but when I suddenly stopped the truck and he heard a rifle shot, he thought I'd shot his wife and then placed her in the back of the truck. He'd been huddled up in my big construction parka with the hood over his head, and he couldn't see what I had put in the back of the truck.

The following morning we went out to check on his car, and we were able to get it started. The couple stayed for the weekend and turned out to be very good customers. During the weekend a couple of us were going out to check our fishing holes, and Mr. Fox suggested we put a dollar in the pot and pick a number for the number of fish we would catch. I picked the number two, because we had been averaging one or two fish per day on our set lines. The customer who was going with me picked the number one and he was sure he would win the pot. Mr. Fox picked zero.

We couldn't believe that he would be so foolish as to pick zero. We checked our set lines and to our surprise we hadn't caught a single fish. When we got back to the lodge and told Mr. Fox that we'd caught nothing, he just smiled and told us he was such a jinx when it came to fishing, that when he was on a charter boat he did not catch any fish, and quite often no one else on the boat did, either.

A couple of weeks later Mr Fox (Jinx) and his wife made reservations to come to the lodge for the weekend, and wanted to go ice fishing with us. We got him outfitted with some winter gear, and again he suggested that we put a couple of bucks into a fishing pool. We drilled several holes in the ice and showed him how to rig his set lines.

We went back to the lodge to warm up and have some of Judy's pie and hot coffee. Several hours later we went back out on snowmachines to check our set lines. We couldn't believe it. None of us had caught a fish, and Jinx won the pool again. I told him the next time he came to the lodge I would guarantee he'd catch some fish. I told him about the secret silver salmon lake, and how good the fishing was in the winter months.

On his next trip to the lodge he came prepared to go fishing. He had outfitted himself with some well-chosen winter gear. Dave Goocey was flying for us, and he also liked to fish. Dave flew Jinx over to the secret lake and he drilled a couple of holes in the ice. Usually, the first person to put his bait in the water would catch a fish almost immediately,

As Jinx put his bait in the water a fish hit and he pulled out a really nice silver salmon. Dave said Jinx was so happy his eyes were full of tears. Jinx and Dave caught a few more fish and Jinx told Dave his wife would not believe this. Dave flew him back to the lodge and Jinx was one happy customer. We took some pictures of Jinx with his fish and we put one on our bulletin board. Mr. Jinx and his wife came to the lodge several more times in the winter, and the came back quite a few times during the summer.

Minnesota Pilot

One winter day we received a letter of inquiry from Gary, who said he was a college instructor in Minnesota. He wanted to know if we had any openings for a pilot; he had several years of experience working for his parents, who owned a resort in Minnesota. He also said he had quite a bit of experience flying floatplanes, and he indicated that his wife wanted to work as a cook's helper.

We answered his letter and told him we were a remote lodge, and at times needed an extra pilot, and we could use a cook's helper. He wrote back that he wanted to apply for the job of pilot and handyman.

Judy and I drove out to the highway to a phone, and we called Gary. We explained to him that the lodge was in a remote location, and although it was beautiful in the summer, winter temperatures could drop to 65 degrees below zero and colder. We told him that the closest town was Glennallen, and it was a 100-mile round trip, that we did not have TV reception, and we were lucky if we could pick up one or two radio stations. We tried to make it clear that the lodge was not a fancy resort.

After we explained all this, he said that was exactly what he wanted. They had a young child and he wanted to raise her in an environment similar to the environment at his folks' resort. I told him Judy and I would talk about it and call him back within the hour. We did, and we figured that if we found the right couple perhaps we could take a few days off now and then. We talked about the couple having a young daughter and decided to allow them to use our bedrooms in the lodge, since the lodge had indoor bathrooms. We'd move out of the lodge into one of our log cabins.

We called Gary and told him that we'd hire him as a pilot and handyman, and his wife as a helper in the kitchen. We also explained that we'd move to a cabin and let them use our quarters in the lodge. He accepted the job and he told us he'd quit his job as a college instructor and drive to the lodge. He expected to be at the lodge around the second week in June.

We eagerly awaited the arrival of our new help, and when Gary arrived he looked around for a few minutes and said that this is what he wanted, and he felt like he was at home. For the next few days Gary and I worked on the rental boats and the big riverboat I used for freighting passengers and equipment around the lake system. Judy received a radio call on our high-frequency radio from our answering service, and it was from Gary's wife. She told Judy she had arrived in Anchorage and wanted Gary to pick her up.

Gary drove into Anchorage later that day, and returned the following day with his beautiful blonde wife and their young daughter. He showed her around the lodge and the premises. We had lunch and visited with them, and Gary and I went back to work grinding down the fiberglass on the riverboat. Just as we started working on the fiberglass, Gary's wife called down to the docks and said, "Gary, the baby needs changing." We looked at each other, but we didn't say anything. We were both covered with itchy fiberglass from grinding on the boat. Gary dusted himself off the best he could and washed his hands in the lake. He went up to the lodge and returned to help me a little while later.

We went back to work and a little later in the day Gary's wife called him again with the same message. "Gary, the baby needs changing." He looked at me in disgust and went back up to the lodge. When he came back down to the docks he told me he needed to take some time off to get some things straightened up.

He returned a couple of days later without his wife and daughter. He said he was sorry he could not continue to work for us, because he felt at home in the lodge. He'd been given an ultimatum—quit the job or find a new wife.

I felt sorry for Gary so I asked him what he planned to do to find work in Alaska. He said he was going to apply with the Anchorage school system, so I told him I'd worked for the Anchorage School District for several years, and I gave him the name of Bob Hall, a friend of mine, who was the personnel director for the school district. I also gave him the names of several principals I'd worked with. We heard he got a job with the school district, but he resigned around Christmastime. Evidently his wife was not happy living in Anchorage.

We were talking to one of our customers about this episode, and she wanted to know more about Gary. We told her as much as we could remember. She just laughed, and we asked what was so funny. She said this person sounded like someone she'd known in college back in Minnesota. The parents of the guy she went to school with owned a nice resort on a lake in Minnesota, and every summer he had his choice of the girls who worked at the resort. He acted the playboy there, and when he got tired of a girl he was dating, he just dumped her. She said if this was the same guy, he got what he deserved in a wife.

New Riverboat

Since it was getting late in the fall of the year I wanted to complete a couple of freighting trips to Lake Susitna before the ice started to form on the lakes. It was relatively quiet around the lodge, so I asked Judy if she wanted to go with me on the trip.

Judy did, and we called Betty Poe, a neighbor, on the CB radio and asked if she would stay at the lodge while we freighted some lumber to Lake Susitna. Betty agreed and when she arrived we told her where we were going to deliver the lumber, and that we planned to be back before dark.

A customer of ours had built several riverboats that were used around the lake. He had designed a new riverboat with a narrow bottom, because he thought it might prove to be a faster boat. He'd asked me to try it out to see what I thought about it. I loaded the lumber into this new boat and put my new 40-horse-power motor on it.

Judy and I decided to take our daughter, AnnMarie, with us so that we could make it a family outing. When we started down the lake it was a beautiful fall day. The air was crisp and the lake was flat calm. We went through the channel that connects Lake Louise and Lake Susitna and continued on our journey. I pointed out several of our customers' cabins and summer homes along the way and we continued to the site where I was to deliver the lumber. Judy helped me unload it, and we started back to the lodge. Lake Susitna was calm and beautiful, so I took the long way around to show Judy and our daughter some other parts of the lake.

We entered the channel that would take us into Lake Louise, and when we entered Lake Louise we were in for a surprise. The lake was so rough the waves were pounding the beach. Lake Louise is eight miles long, and it looked like all the water in the lake was trying to pile up on the beach.

I eased the boat into the waves and figured that since this was the shallow end of the lake, the waves would calm down when I got into deeper water. They didn't. They seemed to get bigger and bigger.

I tried to ease the boat closer to the shoreline, so that we would be out of the wind and the huge waves. The bow was lifting high out of the water, so I told Judy and AnnMarie to move closer to the bow of the boat. They did, and this seemed to help, but the waves were still crashing over the bow of the open boat, and it was starting to fill up with water.

After a while I was able to ease the boat away from the big waves, but it was starting to sink. I told Judy to hold on tight to AnnMarie, because I was going to ram the boat up on the sandy beach to keep it from sinking altogether. I managed to beach the boat, but we were soaking wet and started to get very cold.

We walked up the beach a short distance to the cabin of John Stephensen, one of our customers. I tried the front door, but it was locked. Next I tried several windows, but since it was the end of the summer season, most of the people had locked their cabins for the winter.

Walking around the back of the cabin I found a small window that was unlocked. We boosted AnnMarie, who was three years old, up to the window and told her to go to the front door and unlock it for us. She did and Judy and I looked around for some way to heat the cabin.

There was a propane stove, which we turned on, and Judy found some macaroni. We got undressed and dried off as best we could, but we were still very cold. Judy made some macaroni and that put a little heat back into our bodies. Since we were still cold all three of us got into a bed and pulled all the blankets we could find on top of us.

We slept for quite a while, and when we got up to check weather conditions the wind was still blowing and the lake was too rough for us to get back to the lodge. We didn't have a CB radio with us, and couldn't find one in John's cabin. We knew Betty would be worried about us, but we had no way to contact her. Judy made some more macaroni for dinner, and we went back to bed.

In the morning the wind had stopped blowing but the lake was still rough. With an old coffee can I started to bail out the boat, and got it to float. The motor started after a couple of pulls on the starter rope. Judy warmed up the rest of the macaroni and we had it for breakfast. About that time the lake calmed down enough for us to make a try for it.

Halfway back to the lodge we felt the wind start up again. I headed the boat into a protected cove to wait out this storm. As we headed into the cove we spotted one of our customers, who had a larger boat. He was just starting out to head back for our lodge, so I asked him if we could follow him. We followed in his wake and were able to return to the lodge without any further problems.

We told Betty Poe what had happened and she said she'd been extremely worried, especially since I was trying out a new riverboat. A couple of pilots were staying at the lodge, but she said it was too rough for them to take off to look for us.

Needless to say, I did not purchase the newly designed riverboat, and we did not eat macaroni for quite a few months, but I did buy a portable CB radio.

Psychic

Al Gruchow and I were sitting in the sun room talking about Edward Cayce, Ruth Montgomery, and other people who had written books about psychic phenomena.

A branch of the Mormon Church owned an island on Lake Louise, and they were having their annual summer retreat there. As Al and I were talking about past-life experiences, an attractive redheaded young lady walked through the sun room and paused for a moment. I raised my eyebrows and Al got the message. We both knew we were going to get a lecture on religion from this lady.

The redhead turned around and asked if she could join in on the conversation. We invited her to join us and instead of chastising us she told us about one of her experiences.

When she was a young girl she belonged to the Girl Scouts, and when they danced around the campfire to the beat of the drums she would get so involved in the dance that she'd go into a trance-like state of mind. She also mentioned that for most of her life she'd been deathly afraid of knives, to the point that she would not keep a knife in her home. She had read some of the books by Edward Cayce, and had decided to seek out a psychic to see if that person could help her with her problem.

The psychic she contacted caused her to regress to one of her past lives and she discovered that she had been a beautiful Indian maiden. It was the custom of her tribe to sacrifice a beautiful maiden in order to please their god. In her past life she was chosen as the one to be sacrificed, and she was killed with a sharp knife. She said we could believe what we wanted to believe, but for her the experience with the psychic calmed her fear of knives, and she also understood why she got so involved in campfire dances when she was a Girl Scout. Al and I thanked her for sharing her experience.

In the latter part of August two young doctors flew up to the lodge. They stayed with us that night and said they wanted to go hunting for caribou the next couple of days. I showed them on a map where I had spotted quite a few caribou on the previous day. The next day they had breakfast with us and then flew off looking for the caribou herd.

They came back and had lunch with us, and said they planned to go flying again that afternoon. I asked them where they planned to hunt and they kind of looked at each other and said they were going to Bear Lake.

After they left I told Judy I had a funny feeling about these two hunters, and that I had better get a good night's sleep, because I knew I would have to go looking for them the next day. They did not return before dark, so I went to bed early that night.

After an early breakfast the next morning I told Judy I'd start looking for the doctors around the Bear Lake area. It was not a good day to be flying. The clouds were moving in and the wind was really blowing.

Flying around the Bear Lake area I looked around for their airplane or a signal fire, but I couldn't spot either. The weather was getting rougher and the Super Cub was bouncing around so much I had to focus all my attention on flying the airplane. I headed back to the lodge and planned to call Paul, a friend of ours who owned Tyone Mountain Lodge, to see if we could use his Cessna 180 to look for the two doctors.

I had just landed at the lodge when a plane I did not recognize taxied up to the dock. Sure enough the two doctors got out of the plane, so I asked them what had happened to their airplane. They told me they'd crashed it. When I told them I'd just returned from Bear Lake where I'd been searching for them, they looked at me kind of sheepishly and said they hadn't told me the truth about where they were going to hunt, because they had spotted several trophy caribou in the herd and they didn't want me to know.

I explained to them that I flew practically every day, and since caribou migrate around 20 to 25 miles per day, it was really stupid on their part not to tell me where they had planned to hunt. Lucky for them neither was seriously hurt and they were fortunate that another plane had spotted them and returned them to the lodge.

Sir Lancelot

As noted previously, one summer all our summer help had dark hair. The next year all of them were redheads. This particular year all the help were blond.

We'd had to fire one of the young students who came to work for us because he couldn't get into the habit of getting to work on time or doing any work when he did show up. Since we were short one person we were pleased when a young man showed up and asked if we had any openings for summer help.

There was something different about this young man, who was named Jay. He was very polite and well spoken, and the way he carried himself was different from most young men. Jay wore his hair at shoulder length and it was a beautiful blond color and very well groomed. He looked like Sir Lancelot. Judy and I both interviewed Jay and we explained what we expected of him and what our customers expected of him.

We told him most of our customers were hard-working people, and after putting in a 40-hour week in an office or some other workplace and then driving four or five hours to get to the lodge most of them were in no mood to take any nonsense from anyone. We didn't have a dress code, but we expected our help to be courteous along with being neat and clean.

Jay accepted the job of dock boy. The dock boy's primary job was to keep our rental boats clean, instruct the customers on how to start the outboard motor, and to help our boat customers with their packages and baggage. The dock boys worked for room and board plus tips, and Judy did the laundry for them. They had one day off per week and on that day they were allowed to use one of our rental boats to go fishing or exploring around the lake. We also furnished the gas for the boat and the fishing gear.

Jay jumped right into the routine and he really worked hard helping the customers on the dock. Reggie, our other dock boy, told Jay that perhaps the reason why customers weren't tipping him was his long hair. Jay told us that he did not want to cut his hair, and we said that was his choice.

Several days later Jay was still not getting any tips, so he asked Judy if she would give him a short haircut. Judy had quite a bit of experience cutting hair since she cut mine, the dock boys' and quite often the pilots' hair, and she did a very good job on all of us. Jay could not believe the difference in the way the customers treated him after his haircut. They started to tip him and he seemed to be accepted by them.

I had to dig up part of my water line, so when there were no dock customers Jay and Reggie pitched in to help me with the digging. Neither Reggie nor I wore gloves while using the pick and shovel, so Jay wouldn't wear any gloves either. About the second day of ditch digging I noticed that Jay's hands had several blisters, but he still refused to wear gloves.

Jay told us he lived on the East Coast of the Lower Forty-eight. When we asked him how he got to Alaska he told us he'd hitchhiked, and he wanted to visit with a friend who was attempting to climb Mount McKinley.

Jay wanted to know how he could get in touch with his folks, so that he could tell them where he was going to spend the rest of the summer. We explained to him that we made contact with our answering service in Anchorage twice per day to find out if we had any messages. If someone wanted to talk to us, the answering service patched us through on a radiotelephone hookup. If weather conditions were favorable, the call could be completed. During the conversation callers had to state their message and say "Over," to allow the other person to answer. If weather conditions were not favorable, the conversation turned into utter frustration for both parties.

Jay wrote to his folks and explained all of this to them. A week or so later he got a call from his mom on the high-frequency radio. She wanted to know more about what he was doing and how long he was going to stay at the lodge, and she insisted that she was going to send him some money.

Jay tried to explain to his mom that everything was okay and that he liked what he was doing. He also mentioned that everything she said on the radio could be heard by people all over Alaska. For some reason she did not understand how people all over the state could hear what she was saying.

Later that day Jay asked if I would drive him out to the highway to a regular telephone, so that he could call his mom and explain to her that he was okay, and to be careful of what she said on the radiotelephone.

On our way out Jay told me a little more about where he came from and how he got to Alaska. His father was a lawyer in Philadelphia and his mom lived in Texas, where she raised horses. He'd hitchhiked to Alaska all right, but he didn't ride up the highway in a vehicle. He'd hitched a ride on a small jet owned by the father of one of his friends. His friend had been trying to climb Mount McKinley when he fell and broke his leg. The boy's father had flown up to Alaska to check on his son, and Jay was able to hitch a ride with him.

His whole life his parents had been telling him how hard it was for most people to make a living with their hands, he said. After hearing this story over and over he'd told them he wanted to take a year off from his studies to find out firsthand what they were talking about.

Jay called his mom and explained to her what he was doing and why he was doing it. He also asked her not to send any money and to be careful when she was talking on a radiotelephone. After that call things worked out much better for him. His mom called, but just to ask him how he was doing.

I told Judy about Jay's background, but neither of us told the help or anyone else about it. Jay worked through the entire summer and the fall season, and when we closed the lodge for the month of October he moved to Anchorage to find another job. He was by far one of the best employees we'd ever had at the lodge. He told us he'd learned a lot about using a pick and shovel, and by the end of the season he turned out to be very handy with almost any tool.

When we returned from our vacation at the end of October we contacted the cook who'd worked for us during the summer and asked if she knew what had happened to Jay. She told us she heard he got a job at a tire recapping service in Anchorage, and he continued to work hard to support himself. He'd told her he'd be so tired after work that he went back to his apartment and fell asleep in his work clothes for a while before he had enough energy to get up and get something to eat. We lost track of Jay, but I am quite sure he turned out to be very successful in his adult life.

Mystery

Early in the fall of the year a man we had not previously seen around the lake came to the lodge and told us he was going to rent a cabin on Lake Louise where he was going to stay for the entire winter.

He returned in a week or so and told us he worked for a grocery store in Anchorage and he had a lady friend he was trying to help break away from a dependency on narcotics. He figured that if he could keep her away from her source of drugs perhaps he could help her kick the habit. He thought enough of this lady that he was willing to take off work for the winter months to see if he could help her.

He hauled a lot of groceries and cold-weather gear across the lake to the cabin he was renting, which was about 8 miles from our lodge. His only source of heat in winter would be a wood stove, so he spent a lot of time cutting and splitting wood.

Judy and I had to go to Anchorage for supplies and, as always, told the crew at the lodge to stay out of trouble. We were gone for a couple of days and when we returned several Alaska State Trooper cars were parked in our parking lot.

Bill, who was our pilot at the time, told us that Dean, the grocery store employee, had brought his lady friend and taken her across the lake to the rented cabin in his boat. He'd also brought some of her luggage and more supplies. He left the lady at the cabin and returned to his vehicle to pick up more supplies to haul over to the cabin.

While he was loading the supplies in the boat a storm blew in and the lake became too rough for him to make the trip across the lake. Dean asked Bill to fly him across, but Bill told him the lake was too rough for takeoff or landing, so Dean stayed at the lodge and had supper with the crew. By then it was too late to try and cross the lake, since there were several islands and other obstacles between the lodge and his cabin.

When they got up in the morning the lake had calmed down enough so that he was able to fly Dean over to his cabin. The lady was not there, so Bill and Dean called her name several times, but didn't get an answer. Quite concerned because of strange markings left around the cabin, they started searching for her. Bill flew back to the lodge and used our high-frequency radio to contact the Alaska State Troopers in Glennallen, and they dispatched several officers to investigate the mystery.

The troopers helped Dean with the search, but they could not find the woman, either. They hired Bill to do some flying around the area to see if they might locate her from the air. While Bill was flying the troopers around they spotted a small raft made of a couple of logs, and upon landing next to the raft, they found some of the woman's clothing on the raft.

Bill and the troopers continued their search, and they spotted the body in a shallow part of the lake not far from Dean's cabin. The troopers retrieved the body and brought it back to the lodge. They presumed that the woman had drowned when she tried to swim the 8 miles across the lake. The water was very cold, and the lake very rough. Dean was heartbroken. He had done all he could to help his friend.

Breakfast Cook

We received an application in the mail from a young lady by the name of Katie, who said she was a home economics major in college and wanted to apply for a job as a breakfast cook. She further explained that she had learned a lot about cooking in college, and she was prepared to help us with meal planning and nutrition.

Judy answered her and told her that we did not have a position as breakfast cook, but we used cook's helpers. The cook's helper not only helped in the kitchen, but made beds in the cabins, helped with the laundry, answered the CB and high-frequency radio, and if necessary pumped gas for airplanes or boats.

Katie wrote back to accept the job as breakfast cook and she also mentioned that her mom and dad owned a cabin on Lake Louise and that they were good customers of ours. A few days later Katie's father stopped by on his way to his cabin. We told him about the job inquiry we had received from his daughter, and explained that we had no such position as breakfast cook. He told us he understood what the cook's helper did at our lodge, and he would straighten out his daughter as to the duties of that job if we wanted to hire her. We said we'd hire her if she still wanted the job after he explained to her the various duties of a cook's helper.

A short time later Katie wrote again and said she accepted the job. Katie arrived at the lodge at the start of the summer season. She was well groomed and a nice-looking person. Judy showed her the log cabin next to the lake and told her this was where she would be staying. She also gave her a tour of the kitchen and the building where we kept the freezers.

Katie helped Judy in the kitchen for a couple of days and Judy let her cook breakfast for the dock boys. Reggie was working for us as a dock boy that summer, and he was wise beyond his age. Reggie's dad worked for a large petroleum company and Reggie had traveled all over the world with his parents. When Katie served him breakfast he refused it several times, because he did not like the way his eggs were cooked. Katie was upset about Reggie's actions, but Judy told her that Reggie was just giving her a hard time since she was the cook's new helper.

Things seemed to work out pretty well with Katie until the weekend came around. Everyone was busy with chores and we had several pilots waiting at the dock to get aviation fuel. Judy was busy cooking breakfast, but I didn't see Katie in the kitchen. Judy said she hadn't seen Katie at all. About an hour later Katie came into the lodge for breakfast. When I asked her why she was not helping Judy she told me she had weekends off.

When things calmed down a bit, I told Judy and Katie we needed to have a conference. Judy and I talked to Katie and we asked her to explain to us what her understanding was of the cook's helper position. She said she understood she accepted a job as a breakfast cook, and after breakfast she was free to do what she wanted. She had weekends off and we would furnish a cabin and a boat for her parents to use free of charge.

I could not believe what I was hearing so I asked Katie to repeat it. After she repeated her statement I told her that if she ever found a job like the one she'd just described, I would like to know about it. I'd personally apply for the job.

We could not get this young lady to realize that our busiest time of the week was on the weekend. The heaviest demand for cabin and boat rentals was on the weekends. Katie stayed until the next day, and we mutually agreed that she would return to Anchorage. Later that summer we talked to her father about the problem, and he said he couldn't understand it, because he had talked to Katie about the duties of a cook's helper at our lodge.

Shortly after Katie left we had to get ready for our annual fly-in brunch. Judy was baking cinnamon rolls for the brunch, and the aroma of the cinnamon rolls drifted down to the docks. The dock boys and I headed up to the lodge. Judy said each of us could have one roll, but she didn't want to give out too many because she wanted to have enough on hand for the fly-in brunch.

Several customers begged Judy to sell them a few extra rolls so they could take them to their cabins. Word got out around the lake how good Judy's cinnamon rolls were, so every time Judy made cinnamon rolls she had to make a few extra. She knew there'd be a demand for them.

A young pilot and his dad came to the fly-in brunch. Judy had laid out the eggs, sausage, potatoes, and cinnamon rolls buffet-style. A short while later Judy came into the office and she was crying. I asked her what was wrong and said the young pilot was the first person to go through the buffet line and he took all the eggs she had cooked plus most of the sausage. He'd also come back for a second helping of potatoes and cinnamon rolls. I told her not to get upset at the young man, and take it as a compliment to her cooking.

Later in the day the young man asked me if we had any openings for a pilot. I told him we didn't have an opening at that time, but I would appreciate it if he would give me his name and phone number. When I told Judy he had applied for a job as a pilot she said she didn't think we could afford to feed him, much less pay him a salary.

Brush Your Teeth

In November I was starting to have some minor problems with my 20 KW generator, so I called Alaska Marine in Anchorage to see if they could send a mechanic up to the lodge to check it. Otherwise I'd have to disconnect the generator and haul it to their repair shop in Anchorage.

The person I was talking to checked with the repair shop and he told me that one of the mechanics had a Cessna 180 and would be willing to fly up to the lodge to take a look at my generator. We agreed that I would pay the regular shop rate for the time the mechanic spent flying to and from the lodge, and for the time he spent working on the generator. We also agreed I would furnish room and board for the mechanic and his wife.

The following day the mechanic flew up to the lodge with his wife, and we both went to work on the generator. The mechanic's wife stayed in the lodge and sat by the fireplace and read her book. It took us quite a while to correct the problem with the generator, and after we finished the repair job both of us washed up and sat down by the fireplace to drink a beer.

The mechanic was an avid hunter and fisherman, so we spent quite a bit of time talking about airplanes and hunting and fishing. After a while, his wife opened her coat just a bit and a tiny dog poked its head out from her coat. She looked at the dog and said, "Nobody wants to talk to us, honey, so let's go brush your teeth and go to bed."

The mechanic took the hint and decided to go to bed also. After all the customers had left the lodge, Jan Listoe, a young man who worked for us, went over to our black lab, Bozo, who weighed around 90 pounds. Jan picked up Bozo and looked at her. "Nobody wants to talk to us, honey," he said. "Let's go brush your teeth and go to bed."

Another fly-in customer was a lady who flew up to the lodge on several occasions. One evening I was reading the newspaper by the fireplace and she was sitting fairly close to me. She said something, but I didn't understand what it was. I put down the newspaper and looked at her, and she was talking to her purse. "Excuse me," I said. "Were you talking to me?" She said no, she was talking to her pet box turtle.

I learned that she liked to fly but her husband wouldn't go flying with her, so she took the box turtle with her to have someone or something to talk to on the way. She told me what she fed the turtle, and said she also carried a roll of orange surveyor's tape with her, to tie some tape onto the turtle when she let him outside to go potty. She could find him a lot easier when he was wearing the orange tape.

Another customer who was a female pilot carried a deodorized pet skunk with her while flying because her husband didn't like to fly and she also wanted the company.

Can't Please Them All

Art Watters, one of our former neighbors, had been a truck-stop cook, so he gave Judy quite a few tips on how to prepare food for a large number of customers. He also told her to be prepared for some off-the-wall comments from customers. As an example, he said one of his regulars always told him that his pancakes would make good blowout patches for his truck tires. Another customer always asked for extra pancakes to he could take them home as shingles for the leaky roof on his house.

Joe was one of our teacher friends who came to the lodge almost every weekend to do some ice fishing for burbot, or, as most people called them, fresh-water ling cod. Joe was a true outdoorsman and he had a terrific appetite. He always complimented Judy on the dinner she served, and he especially liked her homemade pies.

Joe and a couple of his buddies finally brought their wives to the lodge for a weekend. He was his usual self, and went out on his snowmachine to do some fishing with his friends. His wife and her friends stayed around the lodge or in their cabins.

Judy served her special lasagna for dinner and as always Joe complimented her on her cooking, and he went back for a second helping. Joe's wife made the comment to him that he didn't ever ask for seconds of her lasagna. Joe didn't say anything; he just finished eating. The next morning Joe and his buddies took off on their snowmachines to check their fishing lines. Joe's wife and her friends came into the lodge a little later to have breakfast.

Joe's wife ordered scrambled eggs, toast, and bacon. Judy cooked their breakfast and served it to the ladies. Joe's wife told

Judy she'd like her bacon cooked a little more. Judy put the bacon back on the grill and she cooked it some more before serving it to Joe's wife again. The lady then told Judy she wanted it crisp. Judy took the bacon back to the grill and put the weight on it to let it cook until it was so crisp that it broke into pieces. She served the bacon again and this time there were no further requests. Joe never said anything about this incident, but he didn't bring his wife back to the lodge again.

A young family from North Dakota came to the lodge one summer to do some fishing for lake trout and grayling. The couple brought their son, who was about six years old, and the husband brought his mother.

The couple and their son were successful in catching some nice lake trout that weighed around 15 pounds, and they also caught some grayling, which is a fish that resembles a very small sailfish, since it has a very large dorsal fin.

Judy had cooked a 30-pound roast for dinner with all the trimmings. I carved the roast so that the customers could select their cut. Judy served the meal family-style so that people could pick out what they wanted to eat as they passed dishes around the table.

Everyone made a selection of the meat, but the young lad did not take any. I asked him if I could cut him a piece of the roast, but before he could answer his grandmother told me he would not eat beef. I told the boy that it was not beef, but the roast was from a buffalo I had shot earlier in the season. He took a piece of the meat and seemed to enjoy eating it. The grandmother got up from the table almost immediately and went back to her cabin. After dinner I asked the boy's dad why his son would not eat beef, and he told me he didn't know why. He'd just decided one day that he did not want to eat beef. When I asked him why his mother had left the table he said his mother had always thought that buffalo were disgusting.

Two tough elderly loggers from Oregon came to the lodge to do some hunting and fishing. Both wore the traditional hickory shirts, suspenders, and romeos, a slipperlike shoe. They had breakfast with us and went fishing for the rest of the day.

The loggers returned in time for dinner and one of them asked Judy what she was cooking for supper. She told them we were having a special treat because she was cooking lingcod. The older and more ornery of the two told her that lingcod was a trash fish and he wouldn't eat any of it. Judy told him that was okay with her, and she gave him a choice of pork chops, steak, or stew. He told her he'd like her to cook him some pork chops.

The harvest table would seat sixteen people. When we sat down to dinner everyone took a helping of Judy's special. She had cut up the lingcod into bite-sized pieces and used a beer batter made with Krustease pancake mix.

The platter of lingcod was almost empty when the younger logger complimented Judy on the meal. He told her that was the best ling cod he had ever eaten. The ornery one said, "Judy probably paid you to say that," to which his friend replied he was glad the older man hadn't eaten any ling cod because now he could have seconds,

The ornery one asked his partner to pass the platter so he could taste one piece. He did, and then he ate several more pieces. Finally he admitted it was some of the best fish he had ever eaten.

Dutch Twins

A pilot who flew for K.L.M., the Dutch airline, and his family were renting a cabin across the lake from our lodge. The family had planned to stay at the lake for a week or so but the pilots of another overseas airline went on strike, and the father of this family was called back to work.

We had never met the pilot or his family until they came to the lodge to ask if we would take care of their two older daughters. The pilot explained that he had to return to work immediately and he could get airline reservations only for himself, his wife, and their three younger children to fly back to Holland. He offered to pay us for the girls' room and board until he could make arrangements for them to fly back home.

We didn't know what to say since we didn't know anything about these people, but they seemed to be in such a desperate situation that we agreed to take care of the girls. They were good-looking 16-year-old twins. We gave the parents our names and the phone number of our answering service in Anchorage.

We were in for a pleasant surprise with these two girls. They not only spoke English but they could speak four other languages. For the first couple of days they kept busy with their schoolwork. They were required to read several books and then translate them into a different language. The students who were working for us at the time were amazed at the amount of schoolwork these two girls had to do over their summer vacation. After the girls caught up on their schoolwork they asked Judy what they could do to help her. Both were good workers, and they helped Judy in the kitchen and entertained our daughter, AnnMarie.

We were starting to get a few European visitors to the lodge, and the girls were a big help in making these customers feel at home, because they could speak their language. At times the girls got so involved in translating for us that they forgot and spoke to us in their native language. We had to remind them we spoke only English.

The twins stayed with us for a couple of weeks that summer. The following year we received a letter from them asking if they could come back to the lodge for a couple of weeks. We told them we'd be glad to have them, since they were like part of our family. The twins pitched in and helped Judy around the lodge and again they did an excellent job in translating for us with our European customers.

Judy's mom and dad were at the lodge when the twins arrived, and they enjoyed talking to them, since they had toured Holland the previous year. I took Judy and her dad along with the twins for a king salmon fishing trip on the Gulkana River. Judy's mom stayed at the lodge and babysat our daughter. We had also arranged to have Betty Poe, a neighbor, stay at the lodge while we went fishing.

We fished for quite a while and none of us could catch anything. I decided to cast ten more times out to a big rock in the middle of the river before I would give up fishing for the day. On the ninth cast something big hit my lure and the battle was on. I knew it was a big fish so I hollered at Judy and the crew to give me a hand.

The fish went from one side of the river to the other, and it made several runs up and down the river. It turned out to be quite a battle; my arms were getting numb, but I couldn't let go of the fishing rod, because every time I gave the fish a little slack it would take off again. Judy's dad got so excited when he saw the big fish that he came running down the slippery bank of the river and fell, hurting his rib cage.

I was still fighting the fish, so Judy and the two girls ran over to help Judy's dad, The fish made one more frantic run across the river and when it turned it headed straight for me. I could hardly reel in the fishing line fast enough to keep up with it. It came across the river so fast that it beached itself on the riverbank in front of me. I had caught a lot of fish, but this fish was something else. It was huge. I got the fish up on the bank and by that time Judy and her father and the twins were standing next to me admiring the big salmon. I cleaned the fish before we left the river, but it was quite a job carrying it back to our vehicle.

We drove to the Alaska Fish and Game office in Glennallen to weigh the fish, but the office was closed. We got Judy's dad cleaned up and stopped in Glennallen to have dinner. When we got back to the lodge several hours later I weighed the fish and it came in at 65 pounds. The fish probably weighed close to 70 pounds when I caught it.

Barney with a large King Salmon

Italian Crew

By our fourth summer at the lodge we had built up a pretty good customer base with several of the overseas airlines. Usually, the pilots and their crews visited the lodge to do a little fishing. When they found out that we were a lodge that catered to families quite a few brought their wives and their families with them to just relax around the lodge or go fishing or boating.

A crew from Italia Airlines came to the lodge for a few days one year. This crew turned out to be the life of the party. They enjoyed themselves and talked to everyone. We had quite a few guests for dinner, and Judy had made seashell spaghetti because for the young kids and for some of the other guests it was easier to eat. When the Italia crew sat down they asked Judy what she was going to serve for dinner. When she told them it was spaghetti they were as happy as could be, but when she put the platter of seashell spaghetti on the table they couldn't believe she called it spaghetti.

The crew ate the "spaghetti" and liked it, but they promised that on their return trip they would bring some real spaghetti and to top it off they promised they'd do all the cooking. A few weeks later they returned and sure enough, they brought a huge box of long spaghetti. They also brought some French bread and a few bottles of wine. Judy had already prepared a meal for the guests at the lodge but the Italian "cooks" wanted our guests to sample their version of real spaghetti. Judy turned the kitchen over to them, and all three started cooking and drinking a little wine. Pretty soon they started to sing and they seemed to enjoy entertaining our guests.

They cooked the spaghetti *al dente*, which means that it was chewy. They added some olive oil, but no red sauce or meat. They served the spaghetti as the first course, and then they served salad and French bread. Between the courses they came around to fill up each person's wine glass.

The meal was excellent and the cooks really entertained our customers. They told us they had enjoyed themselves so much that they promised to return in October, and they'd bring their wives along.

We thanked them for the excellent meal and told them we were closed for the month of October, that it was the month that the lakes started to freeze over, and therefore a good time for us to take a vacation. We also told them that Bill, our pilot, Jan Listoe, and Mel Goodwin, who were all bachelors, would be staying at the lodge during October. That would be just perfect, they said. They'd bring their wives and some extra girls for the bachelors, and they'd do all the cooking.

When we returned after our vacation the lodge was still standing, and it was very neat and clean. There were also a few dollars in the cash register, since the Italia crew insisted on paying for their room and board. Bill, Jan, and Mel told us they had enjoyed hosting the Italia Airline crew, since they'd done most of the cooking and they were a lot of fun to be around.

Japanese

Several Japanese who had climbed Mount McKinley came to the lodge because they had heard about the good fishing. I took them out fishing and they caught a few nice lake trout and some grayling. Not long after that we got an inquiry from a tour leader wanting to know if we would be interested in providing a package deal for a group of twenty Japanese businessmen who wanted to come to the lodge to go fishing.

We agreed on a price for the group and they were due to arrive a few days after the Fourth of July. The crew we had working for us that summer just didn't work out. I had to fire the brother of Judy's kitchen helper and then she quit because I fired her brother. All of this happened during the Fourth of July holiday.

We had to get ready for twenty Japanese businessmen, so I called Marshall Johnson, a friend of ours with a lot of experience cooking for large groups. He agreed to help. Caroline Searcy, a tall and attractive lady of German descent was staying at their cabin with her husband and their family and she also said she'd give us a hand.

The twenty businessmen arrived, and only two spoke to us in English. Judy and I knew a few Japanese phrases, but not enough to carry on a conversation. Through gestures and with our limited use of their language we were able to show them where they were going to sleep.

Their tour guide spoke English, and he was a great help in getting them settled. Judy asked him what they would like to have for supper and he said they preferred American food while they were on this trip.

I told the tour leader that I could take six of his group fishing at one time, and after they caught some fish I would return and take out another group. He said that would work out, because some of them wanted to rest up and be able to take some pictures of the area.

Judy, Caroline, and Marshall put on a really fine roast beef dinner. After dinner the group sat around and talked and took pictures of the trophies in the lodge. The tour leader introduced me to the six fishermen I was going to take fishing the following day. I was surprised that when I spoke to them in the few Japanese phrases I knew they made a very good attempt to speak to me in English.

After breakfast the next morning the six fishermen were ready to go. They came prepared with their hip boots and cameras. Partway down the lake I asked one of the men if he wanted to drive the jet boat. He said he didn't have a license. I told him it was okay since I was the captain and I wanted him to do it.

I handed him my captain's hat and I let him drive the boat. The experience made him very happy, and after a short while he took off my captain's hat, folded his left arm toward his chest and put my hat on his left arm. He bowed and thanked me.

I continued this routine with all the fishermen and some of them got very emotional. We fished for grayling and they proved to be very good fishermen. Every time someone would get a fish on, the rest of them reeled in and walked up and down the beach offering encouragement to the person with the fish on the line.

Of all the fish they caught they wanted to keep only one grayling and one lake trout. When we got back to the lodge they washed off the fish and took some pictures. One of the fishermen brought a pad of ink and an ink roller and some rice paper to the dock. He carefully rolled the ink on the fish and then used the rice paper to take an imprint.

When we were back at the lodge the tour leader explained to me that in Japan a person has to pass a pretty rigid test to get a license to run an outboard motor. That was why it was such an honor for these fishermen to drive my jet boat.

He further explained that the fishermen had taken the ink impression of the fish so that when they got home they could show it to the other members of their fishing group. They asked me to sign and date the imprint to make it official.

We had a small selection of lures that we sold to fishermen for lake trout and grayling. The Japanese purchased all the lures we had, so I had to send our pilot to Anchorage to buy some more. I told the tour leader that each fisherman had to purchase only one or two lures, but he explained to me that this group was part of a larger group that fished all over the world. After this trip these fishermen would go back to their fishing group and talk about their experience in Alaska, and they'd exchange lures with other members of their group, who had fished in Mexico or some other part of the world.

On the second day Judy and her crew cooked lasagna for supper. All the fishermen were busy talking to each other about their trip and having a chance to drive the jet boat. While seated at the dinner table, one of the men handed Caroline one of our big navy coffee mugs, and said something to her in Japanese. Caroline didn't know what he said, but she went to the big coffeepot and filled the cup with coffee. When she gave the cup to the man he looked puzzled. What he'd asked for in his language was a cup of hot water so he could use it for his dehydrated soup mix.

When the tour leader saw what was going on he explained to Caroline what the man wanted. She took the coffee and gave him a clean cup. To show his appreciation for her service he put a small pickled apple into the cup and gave it to her.

Caroline took the mug and the pickled apple into the kitchen and asked Marshall and Judy what she should do with it. Everyone in the kitchen was busy getting ready to serve dinner to the fishermen, so someone suggested that perhaps the man wanted the apple smashed for some reason. Caroline smashed the apple and gave the cup with the squashed apple back to the fisherman.

When he saw what Caroline had done to the gift he'd given her he didn't know what to say or do. Thank goodness the tour guide was able to smooth things out.

After dinner they sat around and talked, and we learned that a lot of them had fished in Alaska for salmon, and had fished in other parts of the world. They were some of the best clients we ever had at the lodge. They were not only good fishermen, but they didn't waste any of the fish they caught.

They were scheduled to leave the following day after breakfast. Before they left they piled gifts on the harvest table for us. They left us a couple of pairs of their hip boots with the split toe. They gave Judy, our daughter, and Caroline beautiful scarves that were wrapped around the small containers they used to carry their lunches. They all thanked me and the staff repeatedly for our hospitality.

After everything was cleaned up all of us collapsed for a short while. Judy thanked Marshall and Caroline for taking the extra time to freshen up the beds for the fishermen each day. Marshall smiled and said that every time they freshened up the beds they found a tip of fifty cents or a dollar on each bed.

Pulling the Docks

For the second year Mike Fawcett and his wife Alma agreed to stay at the lodge for the month of October while we took a vacation. Mike and Alma said they'd come a few days before we closed the lodge to give us a hand putting the rental boats and motors away for the winter.

I had things pretty well organized in the way I took the docks apart and put them up on shore to keep the ice from smashing them during spring breakup. I worked out an agreement with the Mormon Church group. I would maintain their big work barge, replace the flotation and so forth, in exchange for using the barge to install and remove my floating docks.

We assembled the main part of the dock and the finger docks. Then I drove my bucket loader on the barge and loaded the barge with quite a few pieces of galvanized pipe that I used as pilings to stabilize the finger docks.

With a rental boat tied to each side of the barge, Judy and I positioned the barge at the end of the finger dock. After we secured the barge to the main dock, I placed a section of galvanized pipe next to the finger dock, and Judy held it in place while I got back on the bucket loader. I used the hydraulic bucket loader to hammer the piling into the lake bed. Once it was at the right height one of us used a piece of heavy-gauge wire to secure the piling to the finger dock.

To take all the pilings out in October we had to reverse the procedure. Instead of hammering the pilings into the lakebed we had to wrap the chain around each piling and pull it out by using the hydraulic lift on the bucket loader. The work was hard and sometimes dangerous, especially when pulling out the longer pilings that were holding the finger docks in the deeper water.

But it was a lot easier than the year I first installed the new sections of the dock. I didn't have the hydraulic bucket loader then, so I had to get up on a ladder on the end of the wiggly finger dock and drive the piling with a 10-pound sledgehammer. Every now and then I'd miss the piling and instead hit the ladder. If I hit the ladder hard enough it would cause me to fall off and into the cold water.

To remove the pilings I had to use a handyman jack and a piece of chain wrapped around the piling to jack it out of the lakebed.

Mike had never helped me install the docks in spring, nor had he helped me to disassemble them in the fall. This year Mike and Judy helped me with pulling all the pilings, and since it was late in the day I figured we would disassemble the docks in the morning and then pull them up on the beach.

We had a good dinner and since no one was around we all went to bed early. When we got up the next morning the thermometer read 20 degrees below zero. A solid sheet of ice surrounded the docks.

We had breakfast, put on our warm clothes, and went down to the docks to finish their dismantling. The first problem I encountered was the fact that the two rental boats we'd left in the water were now icebound.

I figured that was not going to be a major problem, so I started up the outboard motor on one boat, and Mike started the other one. We had intended to use the rental boats to break the ice around the docks so we could pull them up on the beach. The motors started but they were not pumping water. Evidently, the rubber impellers had frozen, and since they would not pump water we had to shut them down before the engines overheated and seized.

I had pulled my jet boat out of the water the day before, so I told Mike I would tow the jet boat to the campground to launch it and I would use it to break up the ice around the dock and the rental boats.

AnnMarie went with me, and as we got close to the campground I heard a thump up by the engine. I stopped the truck, opened the hood, and for some reason the battery was upside down in the engine compartment. I straightened up the battery and proceeded to the launch area.

AnnMarie helped me launch the jet boat, and we started back to the lodge. We'd gone just a few minutes when I turned around to check the engine. Steam was pouring out of the engine compartment, so I stopped the boat and lifted the engine cover. Both the fresh-water cooling exchangers were cracked. I headed back to the launch area, because I didn't want to burn up the engine.

AnnMarie and I loaded the boat on the trailer and went back to the lodge. Mike had called Bill Poe, who was the local mechanic, and he came to the docks and replaced the frozen impellers in the two boats. We broke some of the ice around the boats with a sledgehammer, and finally we were able to get the rental boats free.

After that we finished breaking the ice with the boats, and finished the day by pulling the docks up on the beach. It had been such a long and frustrating day that I decided to take a hot shower before I went to bed.

I got soaped up and started to rinse myself off when I looked down and saw that the water was not draining out of the shower. I shut off the shower, dried off, and went to bed. I didn't sleep very well because I didn't know what problem was hanging over my head.

We had originally planned to spend three days in Anchorage tying up loose ends before we went on vacation to Hawaii. Now I was down to two days before we had to catch our flight to Hawaii, and I didn't know what problem I was going to encounter with the septic system.

We got up early and I opened the Utilidor I had built to the septic tank. The septic tank had tipped toward the lodge and nothing was draining out. I knew I was running out of time, so I asked Judy to drive up to Glennallen, 50 miles away, to beg, borrow, or bribe the backhoe operator to come to the lodge to dig up and reset the septic tank.

While Judy was gone Mike helped me pump out the septic tank and disconnect the pipes leading to it and out of it. We did as much as we could, and when Judy returned she said our luck must have changed. The backhoe operator had had a cancellation, and he was on his way with the backhoe. The operator dug up the septic tank, and by the end of the day we had everything hooked up and working again.

Mike Fawcett told me before we left on our well-deserved vacation that if I ever heard of anyone complaining about the cost of keeping a boat on our dock to let him know. By the time he'd get done telling them about his recent experience in helping me with the docks they'd probably offer to pay double the regular fee.

We had rented a condo on Maui, and were pleased to find that it was a brand-new building on the beach, with a nice swimming pool on the premises. We did a little sunbathing and swimming, but what we enjoyed the most was that we did not have to talk to anyone. We sat out on the back porch overlooking the ocean and enjoyed the peace and quiet. Every time the manager came by we picked up our stuff and went back into the condo.

After a week of rest and relaxation I went down to the office and spoke to the manager. I told him we were not antisocial, but we had just put in a long and busy season at the lodge, and treasured the peace and quiet of this vacation.

The Voice

An older man and a well-endowed, attractive younger woman wanted to know if we had a vacancy for the night. Judy checked the reservations and told them that the honeymoon cabin was available. The man signed the register and Judy showed them the cabin. It didn't take long for word to spread around the dock that a good-looking lady was staying at the lodge.

Just before Judy served dinner, the lady came to the lodge dressed in pink hot pants and a very low cut blouse. At dinner she sat next to Bill, our young pilot, and introduced herself. She asked Bill what he did, and he told her he was a pilot and handyman at the lodge. To keep the conversation going, Bill asked her what she did for a living, and she said, "I make my living on my back."

Well, that got everyone's attention. She explained that she was a former Apple Blossom Queen, and she did quite a bit of modeling. After dinner she sat around and posed for a couple of camera buffs.

The following morning the gentleman came to the lodge and asked Judy if they could have room service at their cabin. Judy said she was too busy to do that, but she would prepare a tray for him to take to the cabin.

Around noon the lady came to the lodge dressed in a filmy negligee and sat around, and her friend took quite a few pictures of her in different poses. The lady caused quite a stir around the lodge, and we didn't get much work out of the dock boys or our pilot.

Ann, Judy's sister, and her family came to the lodge about the time this couple was getting ready to check out. Again the lady was dressed in a very short pair of pants and a very revealing top. She told us she really appreciated our hospitality, and she wanted to sing a song for us to show her appreciation.

She sat on the end of our harvest table and started to sing. If you have ever heard Edith Bunker sing on *All in the Family* you have an idea of what she sounded like. The screeching was so terrible it would make deaf people hold their ears.

To show our appreciation–because she stopped–we clapped. That was a mistake, for she started to sing us another song. By this time I was down on the floor behind the counter with my fist in my mouth to keep from laughing out loud. Judy's sister ran to the bathroom and closed the door for the same reason.

Thank goodness the lady ended her song, and they left the lodge, I think we all agreed that she should stick to modeling.

Big Red

Larry Yahanian and his son flew up to the lodge for our annual birthday moose hunt. When possible, Larry and I tried to get our moose on my birthday late in August. The weather was cooler, so we didn't have to worry about the meat spoiling. It was also a mini-vacation for Larry's son, since he would have to go back to school a couple of weeks later.

I got up early and when I looked down the docks I saw Big Red's Cessna 180 sitting in the water at the end of our docks at a very weird angle. Just as I started to go to the cabin where Big Red was staying he started walking up to the lodge. When I asked him what happened to his airplane he told me he'd lost several float caps and had foolishly not replaced them.

After breakfast Larry and I went down to the docks to see what we could do to help Big Red. The wind had blown for quite a while during the night, and every time the waves washed over the floats a little more water went into each float. By the time we got up in the morning the only thing that kept the plane from sinking was the small rope Red had used to tie his floatplane to the end of the dock.

Since Red had tied his plane to the end of the dock, the only thing we could do was add more rope from his float to the finger dock. I got the gasoline-operated water pump that we used to pump water out of the boats on the docks, and tried putting the intake end of the hose into the float to pump it out, but the water from the lake kept filling the float faster than we could pump it out.

Al Gruchow and his friend, Bobby, arrived at the lodge a short time later and he suggested that we try using several large truck inner tubes to try to raise the Cessna 180. Al and Bobby had their scuba diving gear with them, and they volunteered to help raise the sinking 180.

By the time those two got their scuba gear on, Larry and I had found several large truck inner tubes plus and inflatable raft. I brought my air compressor and some hose out to the end of the dock. Larry brought the inner tubes and several long sections of rope. Al and Bobby planned to dive into the cold water and attempt to fasten the inner tubes to the underside of each float. If they could secure the inner tubes to the floats, they would attempt to attach the air hose to the valve on each inner tube. We could use the compressor to pump up the inner tubes one at a time to bring the floats to the surface on an even keel.

It took quite a while to get all the inner tubes fastened to the floats. We were quite concerned that if the plane was not brought up evenly it would sink entirely, or sustain damage to the wing that spanned the finger dock.

Al and Bobby tied all the inner tubes and the inflatable raft in place and we took a break to allow the two divers to warm up. Big Red thanked us for trying to help him save his airplane from sinking, and he repeatedly told us he'd pay us for our efforts.

After the break Al and Bobby attached the hose from the compressor to the first inner tube, which started to inflate. They took turns attaching the hose to the different valves, and the floats started to rise up out of the water. It took some time to get all the tubes filled with air, and we were finally successful in getting both floats far enough out of the water to use my water pump.

Red thanked us again and said he didn't have his checkbook with him, but if we made out a bill for him he would turn it over to his insurance company, and if they didn't pay it he would. He worked on the Alaska pipeline, and he could afford to pay the bill.

We figured that the work all of us did was worth at least $500. Red said he thought that was more than fair, because if the plane had sunk at the dock it would have cost a lot more to salvage.

Judy made out a bill for Red, listing the equipment used and the number of man hours involved in raising the sinking Cessna 180. Big Red took off for Anchorage, and we did not hear from him again. I asked several people we knew who worked on the pipeline, and they said he was still working.

A month or so later a Cessna 180 landed and started to tie up on the docks. It was the plane Red owned. I went out to the end of the docks and waited for Red to get out, but the pilot was one of our regular customers. He told me Red had sold him the plane and had moved back to Texas.

Sinking Cessna 180

Raising the Cessnal 180

Minister

It was a relatively mild winter for our area, around 20 to 30 degrees below zero. Around the lakes were lots of caribou, and at the lodge a lot of hunters. Some of them were pilots with their own airplanes, and we also had a lot of people who were using snowmachines on their hunting trips.

One of our customers was a young guy who didn't own a snowmachine and didn't have enough money to rent one, so he walked out to one of the islands on Lake Louise, and just sat there and waited for some caribou to come by.

While he was sitting there, some caribou came fairly close to him, and just about the time he was going to shoot several snowmachines came into view. The drivers stopped and shot at the caribou, but they didn't get any. The caribou were spooked and the young man waited for a while, but no other animals showed up.

He walked back to the lodge and poured himself a cup of coffee, and as he started to sit down by the fireplace I noticed he had a tear in the pocket of his army field jacket. I asked him how he tore his jacket and when he looked down at it he almost fainted. The tear on the left side of his jacket was a bullet hole.

He sat down, visibly shaken. He opened his jacket, and in another pocket over his heart was a copy of his Bible. He told us he was studying to be a minister. I told him I thought he had made a wise choice, and I advised him to stick with the ministry as a career. He didn't blame the hunters for his near-misfortune, because he was dressed in a green field jacket and he was hidden behind some evergreen trees waiting for some caribou to come into view.

The Good Doctor

A doctor and his son came to the lodge in August and wanted to go caribou hunting. I was busy digging a ditch and building a Utilidor for my water line. I told the doctor that our pilot could fly them out to a remote area and he would pick him and his boy up in a few days.

The doctor said that although he had hunted quite a bit he didn't know anything about caribou hunting, and he would like to get a nice caribou for his boy, so I told him if he came back in a couple of days perhaps I'd be able to accompany him and the boy on a hunt, if I got most of my work completed.

They came back a couple of days later. I had just about completed my project and needed a break from the pick-and-shovel routine. I explained to the doctor that I was not a guide, but I would go with him and his son on the trip. He would have to pay the airfare for our pilot to fly us out to Clarence Lake. The pilot would have to make two trips–one to fly us in–and one to bring out our camping gear. The doctor agreed to this, because he wanted his son to have a good hunting experience.

The boy was sixteen years old, and he was excited to be going caribou hunting. We flew out to Clarence Lake and started to set up camp by the lakeshore. We spotted quite a few caribou as we waited for the pilot to return with the rest of our gear.

By the time the pilot came back and we finished setting up camp it was getting pretty late. I cooked supper for all of us and we went to bed pretty early. The next morning we got an early start, and after breakfast we spotted a herd of caribou on the opposite side of the lake.

We used the canoe that was at the lake and took guns and packboards. We paddled across, beached the canoe, and hiked up the hill. At the top we spotted a few caribou but none of them had a decent set of horns. I told the doctor and his son to stay where they were and I would walk around the other side of the hill to see if I could spot a nice set of horns. Just a few minutes after I left them I heard two rifle shots.

When I walked back to where I had left the other two, they were not there. I found them a little farther up the hill, standing by two small caribou they had killed. I was a bit upset so I asked the doctor why he hadn't stayed where I'd told him to stay. He said he got excited when he saw the caribou and decided to shoot them.

We had a discussion about the purpose of this hunt. I told him I was under the impression that he wanted his son to have a chance to shoot a caribou with a nice set of horns. I showed him how to remove the entrails and cut up the caribou so that we could pack them back to the canoe.

We finished cutting up the first caribou, and I told the doctor to start working on the other one. While I was loading meat from the first caribou on each packboard I heard the doctor holler and then start cussing. He'd cut his finger and now he was contaminated. He was worried when he could get back to doing surgery. I cleaned up the minor cut for him and gave him a Band-Aid to put on it.

We had quite a load of meat to pack down to the canoe, so I took the heaviest pack and helped the doctor and his son to get their packs on their backs. Partway down the hill the doctor asked if we could stop for a break. After a few minutes of rest I suggested that perhaps the two of us should switch packs. He agreed to that, and when I put my pack on his back he practically fell over under its weight. We made it to the canoe, unloaded the meat, and went back for the second load. We got all the edible meat back to camp and after supper it didn't take long for all of us to hit the sack.

We were all up early the next day and during breakfast I mentioned to the doctor that I would like to see his boy get a caribou with a nice rack. I also told him I was not happy with the way he had conducted himself the day before, and if he wanted his son to get a nice caribou he would have to follow my instructions.

He agreed to do so, so we took our packboards and rifles and started hiking toward a small group of caribou we'd spotted. We followed a small depression and were able to get fairly close. When we reached a spot where the boy could get a clear shot at a caribou with a nice set of horns, I told him to take his time and take a couple of deep breaths before he shot. About the time the boy was going to pull the trigger, his father shot the caribou. I was so angry I could have punched the man out right there on the spot.

The boy was almost in tears. He couldn't believe what his father had done, and neither could I. I told the doctor what a jerk he was, and since he'd shot the caribou, he could have all the fun of cleaning it out, cutting it up, and packing it back to camp. The boy stayed and helped his dad while I went back to start cleaning up our camp.

About the time the doctor and his son packed all the edible meat to our camp, the pilot flew in and we started to load the plane. I let the other two go back to the lodge on the first trip.

By the time the pilot had picked me and the rest of my gear up and we returned to the lodge, the doctor and his son had left. He had paid the air taxi fee and asked Judy what size boot I wore. When she asked him what he wanted to know that for, he said he felt he screwed up and he would like to make amends by sending me a pair of new Herman survivor boots. He didn't follow through on that promise, either. I never received a new pair of boots from him.

Robbers

Late in October of our first year at the lodge, Judy and I were alone with our daughter. We were enjoying our peace and quiet when I heard a car stop outside. It was dark and it was snowing quite hard.

Two guys got out of the car and came into the lodge. The little guy asked if they could get some dinner. We had eaten ours, but since it was pretty early in the evening Judy asked them what they would like. They both wanted a steak.

These two guys fit the Mafia type as portrayed in any movie I have ever seen on the subject. They were dressed in suits and ties, and both wore long overcoats and hats. My first thought was that we were going to be robbed. So I figured I had better take a close look at these guys and try to remember what they looked like.

I asked the big guy what kind of work he did, and he mumbled something that sounded like we-sell-encyclopedias, but he couldn't pronounce it correctly. The little guy spoke more clearly and said they were working for a new collection agency.

The next thought that came to mind was, "Do we owe anyone money?" I could picture myself or Judy with a smashed thumb or a busted knee. So I hurriedly said, "I don't think we owe anyone any money." I couldn't figure out how these guys found us. We were 160 miles from Anchorage on a good highway, and 20 miles off the main road.

Judy cooked a couple of steaks for them, and while they were eating I wrote down the description of their car and the license number. After they ate dinner they had dessert, and they started to tell us a little more about their business.

The little guy said they were with a company that specialized in bad debt collections. I was still trying to figure out if we owed money to anyone, I asked them about their success rate, and the big guy said it was nearly 100 percent. That impressed me and I told them so, and asked what made them so successful. The big guy said they believed in the "personal touch." Well, he was big enough to handle that part of the job.

The little guy then explained that they were a new agency in Alaska, and they had a lot of success in collecting bad debts owed to hospitals, doctors, and dentists. They charged a certain percentage of the money they collected. If they didn't collect anything from the debtor, there was no cost to the person who'd hired them.

That changed my thought patterns a little, but I still couldn't think of anyone we owed any money. The little guy gave us his card and told us to give him a call if we ever needed his services. They paid their bill and we were relieved when they drove out of the driveway.

It had been a scary situation, since we were 20 miles off the main highway, with no neighbors close by and no telephone. We decided to formulate a plan to thwart a holdup if the situation ever arose. Our bedrooms were above the main part of the lodge, and a loft overlooked the area. We decided to keep a loaded pump-action shotgun in the loft. Since we worked different shifts, we figured that I would be in the bedroom early in the morning while Judy was cooking, and she would be in the bedroom late in the evening until I closed up the lodge. We hoped we'd never have to pull the trigger on that shotgun. The noise of sliding the pump action would probably get the attention of most people.

"Le Chateau"

There was a derelict building next to the road that led to our lodge. The building was in terrible shape; doors and windows were missing, and it was an eyesore. I asked quite a few customers if they knew anything about the building, or where I could locate the owner.

Several people told me it had been a restaurant at one time, but no one could tell me anything about the owner. I finally found out his name from the property tax records, and I wrote to the owner and asked if I could purchase the building. Several months later I received a letter from the owner, who told me he worked on a cruise ship and he was out of the country for months at a time. He wanted to know if I would also purchase the dishes, silverware, and the rest of the equipment that was in the building.

I took several pictures of the structure, and sent them to him with a letter explaining that not only were the dishes and silverware gone, but the doors and windows were also missing and the building was full of trash. It looked like someone had tried to burn it down at one time.

The owner wrote back and said I could have the building if I cleaned up the site. I received the letter before Christmas vacation, and I knew we would have a big crowd for the holidays. I took my chainsaw up to the abandoned building to cut off a small addition attached to the rectangular structure. I cut down through the roof and continued cutting off the walls and the floor of the addition. After jacking up the building and attaching two timbers to the underside to use as skids, I cleaned it out and salvaged what I could from the cut-off addition. Al Gruchow and a couple of other regular customers had made reservations for the New Year's holiday, and when Al and the other guys arrived at the lodge with their families we all agreed it would be a good time to move the building onto the lodge property. I had previously bought a bucket loader and a small Caterpillar, and although the road to the lodge was fairly steep, we figured that with two track vehicles we could move the building without any problem. The building was approximately 20 feet long and 12 feet wide.

We hooked the Caterpillar to one end of the building with a long chain, and used the bucket loader to push on the opposite end. Since there was snow on the ground, the building moved pretty easily. We guided it down the road toward the lodge, and just as we started to climb the small incline to the parking lot both the Caterpillar and the loader spun out.

Not only were we stuck but we had all traffic blocked. Customers could get neither into nor out of the parking lot. We had a lot of sidewalk superintendents offering us advice on how to move the building. We changed the position of the Caterpillar and the bucket loader, and with better traction we were able to move the building to its final resting-place.

The holiday weekend was successful, and after all the guests left I started work on my newly acquired building. I planned to convert it into a combination bunkhouse for twelve people and a meeting room for small groups.

After I leveled up the building I started to work on the inside. I framed in the open space created when I cut off the addition. Neither the walls nor the ceiling had any insulation, and in January the temperature was around 45 degrees below zero, so I decided to install one of my 100,000 BTU oil burner stoves in the building.

Since there were no doors or windows in the building, to some people I must have looked ridiculous standing by a heater trying to keep my hands warm. I installed the doors and windows, and that made the building a little warmer to work in. Then I insulated the walls and ceiling and finished the walls inside with paneling.

When the weather got a little warmer, I built a deck on the front of the building, and installed plywood sheeting on the exterior. Al Gruchow had wired the building for me, so now we had a large bunkhouse and/or meeting room.

We named the building *Le Chateau* and used it for arctic biology classes and several workshops I'd promoted. The ladies from a church group in Glennallen also used it during their "Mothers' Day Off" retreat.

Communication

There were no power or telephone lines to the lake system of Lake Louise, Lake Susitna, and Lake Tyone. Our main system of communication around the three lakes consisted of citizens band radios. It was an easy and inexpensive way to communicate with approximately three hundred privately owned cabins around the lake system. It was also a convenient way to check the weather from one lake to another. Quite often Lake Louise weather would be fine while 8 miles away on Lake Susitna it was quite severe, or conversely, the weather on Susitna and Tyone Lakes might be calm, and on Lake Louise it might be rough.

I had a CB in both of my trucks and I carried a portable CB with me on the Caterpillar while I was working at the sanitary fill or doing maintenance at the Lake Louise airport. I also carried the portable with me on my freighting trips around the lake system. If I could not get through on the portable CB someone around the lake system would relay a message for me. We also had a high-frequency radio at the lodge, which we used to contact our answering service in Anchorage. We called the service twice a day for messages or to make a radiotelephone call. If weather conditions were good, the messages came through pretty clearly. If they weren't, Anchorage couldn't hear us or we couldn't hear them.

Since the radios were on all the time, it was like listening to a soap opera on the radio. One evening at dinnertime a hunter in Yakutat placed a radio call to his girlfriend in California. He kept telling her how much he loved her and he'd say "Over," to allow her to respond. She'd say yes, or something noncommittal. He'd tell her again how much he loved her, followed by "Over," and again he'd get a noncommittal reply. Finally he asked her if some-one else was with her. She hesitated for a moment and said yes. He sounded a bit irritated and said he'd call her the next day.

At dinnertime the following day the same guy in Yakutat placed another radiotelephone call to his girlfriend. The guests at the harvest table wanted to hear the next installment on the saga, so we turned up the volume on the high-frequency radio. He used a different approach this time. He went on and on about how remote Yakutat was, and how bad the weather, and that Yakutat was so far out in the boondocks that he couldn't understand why anyone would want to visit, much less live there.

I had heard enough of his whining and complaining, so I got up from the table and picked up the microphone for the HF radio and said, "Breaker, Breaker, this is the mayor of Yakutat." There was complete silence. That was the last time we heard from the hunter in Yakutat.

Late one night as I was closing down the lodge a call was placed to Anchorage from a remote mining operation. Usually, the report consisted of a lot of numbers and a few brief comments or a request for supplies. Just as I was ready to turn off the HF radio, the person at the mine asked the person in Anchorage if anyone was in the office with him. The answer was no. The miner went into a regular tirade about the SOB of a relative the boss had sent to work at the mine. I was tempted to pick up the mike and tell both of them that all of Alaska was listening to their conversation.

We were also a weather station, and the job required us to observe the clouds, the temperature, and the local weather conditions, and call in the weather report twice a day. The CB and HF radios were on from the time Judy got up in the morning until I went to bed late at night.

For a few months we didn't tell very many of our customers that Judy was a registered nurse. Once the word got out, we were kept busy helping people remove fishhooks that were stuck in fingers and scalps. We tried to help a man who had a heart attack, but we could do nothing to revive him. We were asked to help with knife cuts and a minor gunshot wound, along with several cases of frostbite.

Looking back at our experiences at the lodge for almost seven years, it is clear that we wore ourselves down to a frazzle. Most people take a day or two off per week. At times we didn't have a day off for months at a time. If we had a change in our routine it usually consisted of both of us going to Anchorage for a couple of days to shop for groceries, pick up parts for the outboard motors and/or for the snowmachines, or to pick up building supplies.

A lot of customers through the years, in all seriousness, told us how envious they were of our lifestyle. We were out of the big city and didn't have to punch a time clock or put up with any bosses. They also told us what a great life we had because we had airplanes, boats, and snowmachines to enjoy the great outdoors. The conversation usually ended with, "When I retire I'm going to buy a lodge."

One lady came to the lodge right after the Fourth of July weekend and a day after the twenty Japanese businessmen had left. It was the first time Judy and I had had a chance to sit down and talk to each other about the past week of business. Judy had just vacuumed the lodge and put the last of the sheets in the washing machine and I had just finished changing the oil and the filter in the generator.

The lady had a cup of coffee and said, "Boy, this must be the life. I wish I could buy a lodge." Judy and I just rolled our eyes and Judy asked her why she wanted to buy a lodge. This would be the ideal life, she said. She wouldn't have to cook or do any housework. If we had not been so tired I think we would have taken the time to explain to her what owning a lodge was all about, but instead we both just smiled at her.

A few months later the lady got her wish. Her husband and her father-in-law purchased a lodge on the Glenn Highway. On one of our trips to Anchorage we stopped in to visit with her. She served us some coffee and a piece of pie, and then she ran out to pump gas for a customer. She said she'd like to visit but she had to do the laundry and make up a couple of cabins. We didn't say anything to her about the life of a lodge owner, but I think she was getting the message.

Heart Attacks

After a long and busy weekend I was so tired I couldn't wait to go to bed. I fell asleep almost immediately and slept for a couple of hours. When I woke up I felt a terrible pain in my chest and at the same time the door to the bedroom blew open. It had never done that before, so I figured that perhaps my time had arrived to leave this earth.

I woke Judy up and told her that I thought I was having a heart attack since I was experiencing severe chest pain. Judy got dressed and went to the cabin where Joe Juckel, a friend of ours, was staying. She told him what was happening, and by the time Joe got dressed Judy had the pickup truck parked by the lodge door.

She ran down to cabin No. 1 where the Dutch twins were staying, and asked them to come up to the lodge while she and Joe transported me to the Glennallen hospital. Judy and Joe put a couple of bunk bed mattresses in the back of the truck. Judy sat in back with me while Joe drove the truck to the hospital. I knew the gravel road to the lodge was a bit rough, but riding in the back of the truck I felt every bump.

Joe didn't waste any time driving the 50 miles to the hospital. The doctor there checked me over and gave me the good news that I had not had a heart attack, but he was pretty sure I had a diaphragmatic hernia.

Driving back to the lodge proved to be a more comfortable trip sitting in the front seat rather than in the back. The Dutch girls were glad to see that I was okay, and we thanked them for watching the place. A couple of weeks later I went to our family physician, Dr. Hale, in Anchorage, and had a complete physical. I passed with flying colors.

I'd had a similar experience when I was appointed principal of Chugiak High School. I'd been hired as a teacher and administrative trainee, and was offered the job of principal after only a few months in the school district. I felt I needed to read all the manuals the district published, so on a cold winter day I set out to read all those I had on hand.

I read and took notes for hours on end, and every now and then I had another mug of black coffee. I stayed up and read long after Judy had gone to bed, and to stay awake I drank more black coffee. Finally I went to bed and fell asleep, but a short time later I felt a series of surges in my chest. In my own mind I felt there was no need to wake Judy up, because I thought I was a goner.

When I woke up in the morning my chest was still sore, so I told Judy what had happened during the night. She wasn't very pleased that I hadn't woken her up. We decided I should get an appointment with Dr. Hale so he could check me out.

On the way to see the doctor I reconstructed my previous day's activities. I had read a lot and drunk a few mugs of black coffee. We had a nine-cup coffeepot, and Judy said she's made three pots of coffee that day. She'd had a cup or two, and I had consumed the rest, which amounted to approximately twenty-five mugs of strong black coffee.

After the physical Dr. Hale went over the results, and he couldn't find anything wrong with me. I told him about my activities of the day before, the reading and the consumption of twenty-five mugs of black coffee. He just laughed. I told him I didn't think it was very funny, and besides, it was painful.

But he was laughing in sympathy, because he had done the same thing while he was attending medical school. He explained that what I had done was consume so much coffee that the caffeine stimulated my heart muscle so much that it squeezed all or most of the blood out of my heart, and the heart was struggling to continue to pump more blood. The good doctor strongly recommended that I limit my coffee intake to a maximum of five cups per day.

Brother-in-Law

My sister Marie married a good-looking coal miner by the name of Peter Jyachosky. Pete not only worked a regular shift in the coalmine near Brownsville, Pennsylvania, but he also ran a small dairy farm. He liked to hunt and fish, but with his work schedule he didn't have much time to do either. His typical workday started at 5 a.m., milking the cows, and then it was off to the mine, which was several miles away. After working in the mine and driving back home he would have dinner, milk the cows, and take care of the many chores around the farm.

Pete also raised chickens and a few pigs, and he kept two horses he used for tilling the ground and harvesting the crops. During my high school years, if I was not working at the local gas station I would catch a ride with Pete on Friday afternoon to help him with the farm work. During football season I'd walk to Pete's farm, which was 6 miles away, almost every Saturday morning.

Whenever we had the chance, Pete and his brother, Joe, took me rabbit hunting, raccoon hunting, or deer hunting. I not only enjoyed the outdoor experiences, but it was also a good way for me to stay away from the chaos my father created at home with his excessive drinking. Pete on many occasions gave me the fatherly advice I did not get from my father. He was not only a hard worker, but also a very kind and gentle person.

A couple of years after we purchased the hunting and fishing lodge in Alaska, Pete's daughter, Barbara Ann, wrote to me and asked if I would take her dad hunting and fishing if she paid his airfare to Alaska. Judy and I agreed to have Pete stay with us for his two-week vacation.

I went to Anchorage to pick him up at the airport. When he arrived, he was wearing a white shirt and a coat and tie. When I asked about his attire he told me Barbara Ann had said he had to be well dressed and on his best behavior. He should not eat with his fingers and take the spoon out of his cup before he drank his coffee.

After we picked up his luggage he agreed to take off the coat and tie, since it was quite warm in Anchorage. One of the best places to eat in the city was the Barbecue Pit. It was famous for its barbecued pork and beef. While we were eating a dinner of barbecued ribs Pete couldn't stop smiling. When I asked him what was so funny he said he was doing the opposite of what he'd been told. No coat or tie, and eating with his fingers.

We had a couple of hours to spare, since I had to pick up Nancy, who was Judy's kitchen helper. I showed Pete around Anchorage and he marveled at how beautiful it was with all the flowers blooming. We still had some time to spare, so I invited Pete to have a beer with me. I didn't tell him we were going to a go-go bar. We had a seat and ordered a couple of beers. A few minutes later a nice-looking girl came on the stage and started to dance. It didn't take long before she started removing her clothing. Pete was reluctant to look at the girl at first, but after the second beer he loosened up a bit. After the show he told me that was the first time he'd ever seen a show like that.

We picked up Nancy and drove to the lodge, through the Matanuska Valley and up the mountain past Matanuska Glacier. Although it had been a long day for Pete, he was excited about the sights he was seeing. When we arrived at the lodge Judy was still awake and she made us a snack.

The next day Pete was up bright and early. Judy had picked some of our local blueberries, and she had made blueberry pancakes and eggs for breakfast. Pete said that every time he'd rolled over in bed and saw daylight he thought it was time to get up. After breakfast I showed him around the lodge property and showed him how we generated our own power and supplied water to the lodge.

Pete got to visit with quite a few of our customers and some of the guides who were bringing clients to the lodge. I had hired a backhoe operator to help me enlarge the drain field, so while I was doing that, Bill Niles, a customer of ours, offered to take Pete fishing for lake trout. Bill was an excellent fisherman and since I couldn't take Pete fishing we appreciated the offer. Pete and Bill caught some nice-sized lake trout and Judy cooked the fish for our dinner.

My brother-in-law enjoyed being around Bozo, our black labrador, and the dog enjoyed Pete, because he would keep throwing sticks for Bozo to retrieve. I had to deliver some lumber to Lake Susitna for a customer, so I invited Pete to go along for the boat ride. We took Bozo with us, and a shotgun. Every time we passed some ducks on our freighting trip Bozo started to shiver and shake with excitement.

After we delivered the lumber we started to look for some ducks. Pete had hunted for most of his life with a shotgun, but he had never hunted for ducks. We spotted some mallards in a small bay and managed to park the boat and get close enough for Pete to get a shot at the ducks. He got two, and Bozo retrieved them for us.

We got a couple more ducks on the way back to the lodge, and Bozo retrieved them also. We cleaned the ducks and Judy cooked them for our supper. When the weekend came, Pete couldn't believe Judy had baked thirty-eight assorted apple, blueberry, and cherry pies, and after the weekend was over he couldn't believe they were all gone.

After the weekend I had to do some backfilling of gravel around the lodge, so Pete helped me with the job. When we finished I told him to put on his hip boots and get ready to go moose hunting. We had sighted in our rifles earlier, so Pete was familiar with the rifle he was going to use. He was really familiar with the 30.06, because he had helped me pick it out when I first went deer hunting with him quite a few years ago.

As we were getting ready to go hunting, Pete said he couldn't believe what we were doing. When I asked him what he meant by that, he told me, "Back in Pennsylvania we would plan for months to go deer hunting. In Alaska we work part of the day and then go hunting." Bill–"Wonderful Willie" we called him–was flying for us at this time. Bill was a former executive for a major car manufacturing corporation and he had accepted the job of pilot and handyman just to take a break from the fast-paced corporate life. Bill owned his own airplane and he was also a flight instructor.

We had just gone through a gut-wrenching experience with another pilot, who crashed a Cessna 180 we were leasing from Al-Mar leasing company. Before I hired Wonderful Willie I took him to the toughest flight examiner I could find in Anchorage. We had just purchased a newly rebuilt Cessna 180 with only twenty hours on the engine. The examiner proved to be as tough as ever, but Wonderful Willie passed the test with flying colors.

Wonderful Willie flew us around for a while and we spotted a nice bull moose next to a good-sized lake. We landed on a nearby lake, and Pete and I stalked the moose until we got into a position where Pete could get a clear shot. Pete took his time and he killed the moose with one shot. When he got up to the moose he couldn't get over how big it was. He kept comparing it to the size of some of the cows he'd owned.

Pete was an old hand at butchering so it didn't take long for us to clean out the entrails and cut up the meat. We packed the meat to the airplane and our pilot flew it back to the lodge. While we were waiting for the pilot to return, Pete said he felt like he had died and gone to heaven.

For years and years he'd read in various hunting magazines about people hunting in Alaska. He'd always wished for the opportunity to hunt in Alaska, but he knew he couldn't afford it. Now he was hunting and fishing in Alaska and he had a hard time believing he was actually doing it. I told him that if anyone deserved it, he did, because he'd worked hard all his life.

When we got back to the lodge I cut up the tender back straps of the moose and Judy cooked them for our supper along with some fresh vegetables from our greenhouse garden.

We rested up for a day and I told Pete we were going caribou hunting at Clarence Lake the next day. We had twenty-four people booked to fly out to different lakes to go hunting for moose and caribou. A group of long-haul truck drivers from Colorado came to hunt with us again. We had worked with a few of these hunters before, and they were a fun bunch of guys to have around. Wonderful Willie was putting the Cessna 180 to good use, so when we had a break between hunting parties he flew us to Clarence Lake. We unpacked our gear and Wonderful Willie flew back to the lodge. We planned to stay at the lake for two days to give us enough time to get a nice caribou for Pete.

We set up the tent and rolled out the sleeping bags. Pete had never slept in a sleeping bag, so this was another first for him. It was around suppertime, so he asked what we were going to eat. When I showed him a couple of boxes of dehydrated food he just laughed. There wasn't enough food in those boxes to feed a chicken, he said.

Pete got quite a surprise as the ingredients started to swell to their normal size. I am not much of a cook, but we had enough for dinner, plus we had dessert.

The next morning after an early breakfast we spotted a nice herd of caribou quite a distance from our camping spot. We decided on a route that would allow us to intersect the moving band of caribou. I put on my packboard and asked Pete to do the same.

We hiked for quite a while before we got close to the herd, which moved to an area that was pretty open, so as we got closer, we didn't have any brush to hide behind.

The herd was too far away for us to get a decent shot at them, so I suggested that we leave our packboards, cradle our rifles close to our chests, and try rolling down the hill to get closer to the caribou. Partway down the hill both of us started laughing because we looked ridiculous rolling down the hill through the blueberry bushes.

We stayed put for a while until we stopped laughing, and ate a few blueberries. We started our rolling approach again and by now we were covered with blueberry stains. However, we got close enough for Pete to get a nice caribou, and then the work started. After we cleaned out the caribou we tied the meat on our backpacks and walked back to our camp.

We stashed the packs and the meat a little way from our camp just in case a grizzly bear decided he wanted it more than we did. After dinner we decided not to sleep in the tent just in case we got a visit from a grizzly. As a further precaution we tied a couple of empty cans to each packboard to give us some warning of an unwanted visitor.

Wonderful Willie came to pick us up early the next morning and we were able to pack everything into the 180. We took a different route to the lodge to show Pete some of the Alaska scenery.

When we got back to the lodge Judy told me things were going okay. Wonderful Willie had flown out twenty-two of the twenty-four hunters we had scheduled. Judy cooked us some of the caribou for dinner, and Pete loved it.

Early the next morning Wonderful Willie was scheduled to move the Colorado group of hunters to another lake, which I had named "Dumbbell Lake," because from the air it looked like a dumbbell. After breakfast I went out to the highway to pick up our mail and when I returned Judy said Wonderful Willie had called on the Cessna 180 high-frequency radio, and he wanted to talk to me. It seemed strange, because the HF in the 180 rarely worked. When I called him back he told me he needed some help getting the 180 off a sandbar. I told him to drain out most of the fuel to lighten the load, leave just enough in the tank to make it back to the lodge, and ask the hunters to help push the 180 off the sandbar. He said he'd tried all that and it didn't work. He wanted me to fly over and give him a hand.

I knew where the lake was because I had flown supplies there for a previous hunt, and I asked a customer to go with me to give us a hand. When I approached the lake I couldn't believe my eyes. My brand-new Cessna 180 was not stuck on a sandbar–it was pancaked on the hill next to the lake. My emotions ran the full gamut; I didn't know what to think. All I hoped and prayed for was that no one got killed or seriously hurt.

I landed and taxied up the beach and Wonderful Willie helped me tie up the plane. He tried to explain what had happened, but I told him all I wanted to know was if anybody got hurt. His reply was that he was the only one in the plane when it crashed, and he wasn't hurt.

The plane was a mess. The floats were damaged, the wings and the prop bent. Wonderful Willie told me that when he took off everything worked okay but the plane stalled as he started to clear the bank by the lake. Now the problems started to escalate; not only was the 180 out of commission, but we had twenty-two hunters out in the bush that we had to get back to the lodge, with whatever game they had harvested. We took the survival gear out of the 180 and I flew back to the lodge with Wonderful Willie. I asked him several times if he felt he could continue flying and he said he was okay, but he felt bad because he crashed the plane.

He flew back to Dumbbell Lake and picked up the customer who'd flown in with me. I called the FAA and reported the accident; they promised to send someone out to investigate. Wonderful Willie used my Super Cub to continue flying hunters back to the lodge. Since I was busy with the accident, one of our customers offered to take Pete to Anchorage to catch his flight home to Pittsburgh. Pete thanked both of us for giving him the opportunity to hunt and fish in Alaska. For him it was a dream come true.

On the second day that Wonderful Willie flew my Super Cub he was overdue on his flight back to the lodge. I didn't have a HF radio in the Cub so we had no communication with him. About two hours later a Cessna 185 taxied up to the dock. I was on the dock at the time and just as I was going to ask the pilot if he had spotted my Super Cub, Wonderful Willie got out of the airplane.

I took one look at him and knew something bad had happened. As he stepped off the floatplane and onto the dock I had my fist doubled up. I was glad he was walking and talking, but I felt a great urge to pound the hell out of him right there on the dock. He was in tears as he explained to me that he had rolled over my Super Cub in a lake.

I was dumbfounded. We had worked very hard building up our air taxi business, and in three days this superqualified pilot/instructor had crashed my entire fleet of airplanes. I told him I was going to take a walk to calm down, and I would talk to him when I got back.

He waited for me in my workshop, and when I returned he tearfully explained that as he started to take off a strong wind had come up and started to lift one wing of the airplane. He knew he should have added power and turned into the wind, but he also remembered that he'd screwed up the 180, so to be more careful he cut the power and the strong wind rolled over the Super Cub. Thank goodness he was close to shore and he was able to get out of the plane and swim to shore.

He said he was very sorry for wrecking both of my airplanes, and he knew I had no insurance on the Super Cub, so he would pay for the damage to that plane. We walked up to the lodge and he explained to Judy what had happened.

We still had to retrieve all the hunters from the bush. I went out to the highway to phone several guides I knew, but they were all busy with their clients. Hank Rust at Rust's Flying Service promised to bring up two airplanes to help.

Hank and Kenny, one of his pilots, flew up to the lodge and brought all our hunters and their harvested game back to the lodge. We had to make several more phone calls to cancel the rest of the hunters who had planned to use our air taxi service.

Hank told me who I could contact to retrieve both aircraft. It took the salvage crew a day to get the Super Cub rolled over. Once the plane was rolled over they drained the oil out of the engine and drained the fuel. They put new oil in the engine and fresh gas in one of the wing tanks, and checked the plane over. After taxiing the Cub around the lake for a while and finding it performed okay, the pilot flew it back to the lodge.

The FAA inspected the 180 crash, and determined that perhaps the yoke had malfunctioned. That made me feel a little better, but by then I had decided that I would sell both airplanes and the air taxi permit. The salvage crew worked on the 180 for quite a while, and they were able to fly it back to the lodge also. They hauled both airplanes to Anchorage on trailers, and we had them completely rebuilt. Shortly after they were overhauled we sold both.

Wonderful Willie stayed at the lodge and helped us until we went on vacation in October. After we returned he left, and again he told us he would pay for the repairs on the Super Cub. He left a forwarding address and when I got the repair bill I sent him a copy.

We waited for months, but we received no check from him. I called one of his relatives in Anchorage, who was good enough to give me a new phone number for Wonderful Willie, but I could never get anyone to answer that phone. Several months went by and one day we saw Wonderful Willie coming out of a parking lot in Anchorage and head for the Captain Cook hotel, where we were staying. I confronted him and asked him why he hadn't sent us a check. He didn't really have a good answer, but he asked me what it would take to get me off his back. I told him that for a check for five hundred dollars right now I would call it square. He gave me the check, and that was the last we ever saw of Wonderful Willie.

We sold the air taxi permit to two brothers, Fred and Glenn Laufenberger, who were in the construction business. They rented a cabin from us and continued the air taxi business at Lake Louise, and they also opened an office in Bethel, Alaska.

Transition

Now that we were out of the air taxi business we started to promote our place as a family-oriented lodge rather than just as a hunting and fishing lodge.

With the help of Al Gruchow we promoted a twelve-hour marathon snowmachine race on Lake Louise, and several family-type snowmachine races. One race we had a lot of fun with involved a husband-wife or boyfriend-girlfriend team. We would blindfold the husband or boyfriend who drove the snowmachine, and it was up to the lady passenger to give the driver directions to navigate around the obstacle course I had laid out on the lake. The snowmachine with the best navigating time won the prize. Most couples had a lot of fun with the race, but a few guys got a bit angry with their partners because they couldn't judge distances very well or couldn't make up their minds whether the driver should turn left or right.

Another race we sponsored involved the entire family. We blew up a bunch of balloons and turned them loose on the lake. The passenger who collected the most unbroken balloons after a set period of time won the prize. The prizes ranged from a free tank of snowmachine gas to a free weekend at the lodge.

A popular race had the passenger on the snowmachine holding a hard-boiled egg on a teaspoon while the driver maneuvered around the obstacle course. The team that crossed the finish line first with the egg on the spoon won the race.

As snowmachines became more popular, more families purchased more than one. The cabin owners around the lakes now had access to their cabins throughout the winter and this also helped bring business to the lodge.

The transition from a hunting and fishing lodge to a family-type lodge went very smoothly. Word spread that we catered to families, and that Judy was putting out some great meals. Since we were open on all holidays, a lot of families came to the lodge to celebrate Thanksgiving or Christmas.

One year on Christmas day we had twenty-one stockings and a pair of leotards hanging by the counter. The customers were good about putting small items in all the stockings, and of course, Santa added a few more gifts.

The customers participated with our family in putting up the tree, and they also helped decorate it. One of our lady customers from Anchorage had enjoyed Christmas at the lodge the year before. The following year she invited a friend from Michigan to celebrate Christmas with her at the lodge.

We celebrated Christmas with our customers, but we also reserved some family time to open our personal gifts on Christmas Eve. An older couple was working for us one year during the Christmas season. Everyone enjoyed giving a small gift, but this couple sat there like two bumps on a log. After the customers left they said they believed in Christmas but they didn't give gifts. When we asked them why the lady told us that when their daughter was growing up they'd told her about Santa Claus, and that the gifts came from him. When she got older she told her mother she knew Santa Claus was not real, and wanted to know why her mother had lied to her. She didn't know what to say to her daughter, but from then on they had not participated in giving gifts at Christmas.

Although we were not in the air taxi business anymore, a lot of pilots and guides still used our lodge as a base camp for their customers. During the hunting season we often had as many as seven guides working with us. Several would have their wives pick up their clients at the Anchorage International Airport and transport the clients to the lodge. If the guides were held up by bad weather or by some other problem, we furnished room and board for their clients. If the client liked to fish we provided fishing gear and a boat.

To take up the slack of not having the air taxi business we also promoted the lodge as a conference center. On several occasions we conducted workshops that included classes in arctic biology and psychology. When the construction of the Alaska oil pipeline started, several of our customers handed out our lodge brochures to the people they worked with on the pipeline, and that also helped promote our business.

During pipeline construction I added a couple of lines to our brochure. It now read, "We fought like hell for Alyeska's dream—now it's your turn to keep Evergreen Lodge green." It didn't take long for these brochures to catch the eye of some of the people in management.

We got a visit from a couple of men from the management team of Alyeska Pipeline Service Company and they wanted to book the entire lodge for the Labor Day weekend. We asked them what type of meals they wanted, and they specified 2-inch steaks. They would furnish the grill, which was made out of a piece of the pipeline.

They rented all the cabins and fishing boats, and they said they'd bring a piano with them and a piano player. We told them we had a beer and wine license, and that was fine with them. People who wanted something different could furnish their own.

Marshall Johnson had helped Judy with several other events and offered to help with this one. Judy and Marshall put their heads together and decided what they were going to serve this select group of people for breakfast, lunch, and dinner over the holiday weekend. I put up the volleyball net and set up an area for pitching horseshoes. We made sure the boats were extra clean and all the fishing gear was in top shape. We had catered to smaller groups before this, but not a group as large as this one.

Labor Day came and we had beautiful weather. The group started to arrive and, as promised, they brought a piano and a good-looking pianist. They also brought two barbecue grills. After a couple of rounds of drinks, the lady played the piano and everyone sang songs.

Judy, Marshall, and two of the men from Alyeska grilled the 2-inch steaks and we all had a fantastic dinner. Judy served her famous cheesecake jubilee for dessert, and everyone raved about it.

The music and singing went on for quite a while and then everyone was off to bed. The next morning Judy and Marshall served a combination of eggs, bacon, and toast, or eggs with pancakes.

After breakfast a lot of the men and women went fishing, and some of them played volleyball. A few hours later a helicopter landed in the parking lot and the pilot wanted to know how he could find the superintendent. I told him the general area where I thought the group was fishing, and he took off immediately.

In a very short while all the boats came back to the lodge and we were told there was a disturbance at Pump Station 6, and all personnel had to return to Glennallen as soon as possible. A couple of days later two men from Alyeska came to the lodge and paid for the entire weekend of boat rentals plus room and board. They told us there had been a ruckus at the mess hall that required their immediate attention.

Tiger

When we bought the lodge Thill and Ella Wallace, friends of ours from Chugiak, gave our daughter two small kittens. AnnMarie named them Muffin and Puffin. The kittens had fun romping around the outside of the lodge, and our black labrador Bozo tolerated them. The kittens were around the lodge for a week or so, and one of them turned up missing. The following week the second one disappeared. We had a lot of bald eagles around the area, and often wondered if they took our kittens.

Marshall Johnson heard about the missing kittens and picked up a kitten at the pound, which he brought to the lodge for our daughter. AnnMarie named the kitten Tiger, and since we had lost two kittens all of us kept a closer watch on Tiger, especially when the bald eagles were around.

Tiger was pretty much an outdoor cat, but we allowed her to stay in the lodge at night. Just before turning off the lights I put Tiger outside to take care of her needs. It took me only a few minutes to lock the doors and turn off the lights. By the time I walked across the lodge and up the steps to our bedroom, Tiger had taken care of her business, run up the ladder and across the roof, and she'd sit at our bedroom window scratching at the screen to make sure I let her back into the lodge.

Just about the time I fell asleep Tiger would wake me up by running around the lodge. She jumped up on one of the couches, jumped off and shot across the room to jump on another couch. After that she ran across the lodge again and up the steps to our bedroom. She hit the tassel on the drapes and dashed back down the steps to the lodge. The cat weighed only 8 to 10 pounds, but it sounded like an elephant running around the lodge.

Mike Fawcett and his wife, Alma, owned a dachshund named Rocky, and when they came to visit or help us at the lodge they always brought Rocky with them. Tiger got along with our black labrador, Bozo, and quite often she would sleep on top of Bozo. But Rocky was a different story, perhaps because he was a lot smaller than Bozo.

Tiger loved to play games with Rocky. If Rocky was in the lodge, Tiger would hide under one of the chairs under the harvest table and patiently wait for Rocky to walk by. Just as the dog walked by the chair Tiger pounced on his back and Rocky would run to find Alma or Mike. Tiger didn't hurt Rocky, but she sure liked to harass him.

When we sold the lodge Tiger and Bozo moved to Anchorage with us, and when we moved to Sequim, Washington, we shipped them by air to Seattle. Judy's brother, Ward, picked them up and kept them till we arrived.

Sale of the Lodge

The lodge was doing well as a business, especially with the influx of a lot of new people who worked on the Alaska pipeline project.

We decided to put the lodge up for sale, and we placed an ad in the Wall Street Journal. Among the seventy-five inquiries we received was one from a group of Japanese businessmen. Some of the inquiries were very interesting. One was from a gentleman in Pennsylvania who wanted to trade us his funeral home for the lodge. We didn't accept his offer.

A man from Oregon in a very long letter requested more information on the location of the lodge, and he had a lot of questions about the lodge operation. We answered all his questions and he wrote back offering to trade us his new and used car business in Oregon. He said he was getting a divorce and wanted to start a new life and a new business. He also offered his wife as part of the trade. We wrote and told him we were not willing to trade.

A nice letter of inquiry came from a couple in Jackson Hole, Wyoming. They owned a gift store and wanted to relocate to Alaska. We exchanged a few letters, and they were interested enough to fly to Anchorage, and they drove up to visit with us. They spent several days looking over the lodge and talking to us about its operation. We came close to trading businesses with them, but when they told us it got almost as cold in Jackson Hole as it did in Alaska we decided not to trade.

While all these inquiries were coming in, I was meeting with a group of Japanese businessmen on a fairly regular basis. We met at the Captain Cook hotel in Anchorage; usually there were six Japanese and a local who acted as an interpreter. I was led to believe that the Japanese did not understand or speak English.

I went to the first meeting with them by myself. It was a very gracious meeting, and everyone was introduced to me. The interpreter told me the group was very interested in purchasing the lodge, and they wanted to know if I would agree to a property exchange as part of the deal. I told them it depended on where the property was located, and how much it was worth. The interpreter conveyed my answer to the group and we agreed to meet again in a few weeks.

When the interpreter called on our radiotelephone to set up another meeting to discuss the purchase of the lodge we agreed on a date, and this time I took Judy with me. The meeting was cordial but strained; the Japanese did not appear to be comfortable with Judy present. Through the interpreter we discussed a few more ideas on property exchanges and we decided to meet again in the near future.

The meetings went on for quite a few months before I had the opportunity to talk to Mr. Seki, in English, about the operation of the lodge. The Japanese did not plan to operate the lodge as a public business; they wanted to use it exclusively for Japanese customers who were taking a bus tour that started in Anchorage and took them through the Matanuska Valley past Matanuska Glacier to Evergreen Lodge. The group would then spend a day or so at the lodge and they they'd proceed by bus to Valdez. There they'd board the Alaska ferry and travel past Columbia Glacier to Whittier and from there by train to Anchorage. After this meeting Mr. Seki said the group would like to meet again in a few weeks.

I had to go to the hospital for some minor surgery so I plowed a long runway on the ice in front of the lodge, and lined the sides with evergreen branches to give the pilots some depth perception.

The day after my surgery Judy told me that a couple of the Japanese men were in Anchorage and they wanted to inspect the lodge property again. Since I wouldn't be able to give them the tour, I asked Judy to arrange a flight with a local air taxi service. She made the arrangements and accompanied the Japanese to Lake

Louise. They inspected the lodge and the premises.

Mike and Alma were watching the lodge for us, and they offered to make lunch or a snack for the group, but the spokesmen said they were in a hurry to get back to Anchorage. When Judy visited me in the hospital that night she said the plane ride back and forth had been very quiet. No one said a word.

Negotiations with the Japanese group escalated, and with the help of our attorney, Brian Brundin, and Steve Hasagawa, our banker, we agreed to the property exchange and the amount of cash that was to be paid. Mr. Seki agreed to meet us at the bank the next day to close the deal.

The next morning Judy, Brian Brundin, and I met at the bank. Steve Hasagawa came forward to meet us and he didn't look very happy. He told us he was worried about the well being of Mr. Seki. Since the oil embargo had been announced, the Japanese government would not allow large sums of money to be taken out of the country, and Steve said the transaction could not take place today because Mr. Seki and his friends had not transferred their funds from the Japanese to the Anchorage bank. Steve was worried that Mr. Seki would be very embarrassed and to save face he might do some harm to himself.

All of us were disappointed that the sale didn't go through, especially after the long months of negotiations. That was the last we heard of Mr. Seki and his group.

In the meantime the word was out that the lodge was for sale, and we were bombarded with questions from our customers on who was going to buy it, and what the new owner was going to do with the lodge.

Several customers were contractors and they had built rental fourplexes they offered in trade for the lodge, but I didn't want to trade for any rentals, because we'd had a very bad experience with the first duplex we purchased. I'd come close to going to jail for threatening to throw the tenant through a window for his non-payment of rent. We were finally able to get rid of that tenant, but when I saw what he had done to my brand-new duplex I knew I'd have gone to jail for more than just throwing him out the window.

This demented person smeared everything you can imagine all through the cabinets and drawers in the kitchen. He left a huge cardboard box in the living room with a lot of his kid's soiled diapers in it. He knew the box was too big to go through the door, and we'd have to dismantle the box and remove the contents.

The military finally gave us some help and they gave him an undesirable discharge and sent him back to the States. For six months of rent we received a worn-out electric can opener and a set of outdated encyclopedias.

We looked over and considered quite a few of the offers we received, and decided to sell the lodge to a group of local people we had previously met. The group consisted of Jack and Jan Hanson and Hal Post. Jack and Jan worked in Anchorage and I'd know Hal Post when I worked for the Anchorage School District.

We moved to Anchorage and I put the finishing touches on a Justice cedar home we'd taken in trade on the lodge. We stayed in Anchorage for a little more than a year to make sure the lodge was doing okay, because we had a long-term financial interest in it. After a year in Anchorage we decided that if we were ever going to leave Alaska this would be the time to do it. Our daughter was still in grade school and the property values around Anchorage had really escalated.

We'd heard a lot about Sequim, Washington, from some of our customers. We visited Sequim and liked what we saw, because in some ways it reminded us of Alaska. We purchased a 10-acre farm and moved to Sequim.

During the first year there we had twenty or more of our former customers call us when they visited Sequim or the surrounding area. People visited us on almost all major holidays, including Christmas and New Year's Day. I told Judy we should call the farm "Evergreen Lodge South."

After a year on the farm in Sequim we decided we needed something to keep us busy. I found a department store and a 20,000-square-foot building for sale in historic Port Townsend. We sold the farm and purchased the department store and the building and moved to Port Townsend.